Constantine and the Council of Nicaea, 325 C.E.

REACTING CONSORTIUM PRESS

This book is a "reacting" game. Reacting games are interactive role-playing games in which you, the student, are responsible for your own learning. They are used at more than 300 colleges and universities in the United States and abroad. Reacting Consortium Press is a publishing program of the Reacting Consortium, the association of schools that use reacting games. For more information, visit http://reactingconsortium.org.

Constantine and the Council of Nicaea, 325 C.E.

DEFINING ORTHODOXY AND HERESY IN CHRISTIANITY

DAVID E. HENDERSON AND
FRANK KIRKPATRICK

REACTING
CONSORTIUM PRESS

© 2016 David E. Henderson and Frank Kirkpatrick
All rights reserved
Set in Utopia and The Sans
by Westchester Publishing Services
Manufactured in the United States of America

The University of North Carolina Press has been a
member of the Green Press Initiative since 2003.

ISBN 978-1-4696-3141-7 (pbk.: alk. paper)
ISBN 978-1-4696-3142-4 (ebook)

Cover image: Fresco of Emperor Constantine speaking on the
council in Nicaea by Juan de Valdes Leal (1622–1690), in church
Hospital de los Venerables Sacerdotes, Seville, Spain
(Photo by Renáta Sedmáková; courtesy of Adobe Stock).

Distributed by
The University of North Carolina Press
116 South Boundary Street
Chapel Hill, NC 27514-3808
1-800-848-6224
www.uncpress.unc.edu

Contents

Tables

Map

Constantine and the Council of Nicaea, 325 C.E.

1

Introduction

"The winners write the history" has probably never been truer than in the case of the development of Christianity. The Council of Nicaea is in many respects the founding of the Christian church as we know it. Constantine used the Greek word KATHOLIKON (ΚΑΘΟΛΙΚΕ) to mean all-encompassing or universal, and the Roman Catholic Church takes its name from this term. However, at the time of the Council of Nicaea, the goal was to form a single, unified KATHOLIKON Church, and the Christian church was in fact mostly unified until the split between the Western and Eastern branches in the second millennium. In this text, the word Catholic is used to mean universal and refers to the Christian church throughout the world that Constantine helped establish.

The Council of Nicaea was the first grand council to attempt to bring bishops from the entire Roman Empire together to make decisions on issues of theology and church policy. The precedent was set for bishops to make such decisions, and the stage was set for the development of a strongly hierarchical church structure. As the Church developed, it worked to eliminate documents and beliefs that did not fit the prevailing doctrines. Once these doctrines were ratified through councils of the Church, it became difficult for the official story of how the reigning orthodox views came into existence to be subjected to historical analysis. Such analysis would have revealed that the story of the development of doctrine at the Council of Nicaea, for example, involved actions and events that might strike contemporary readers as less than fully noble. Any threat to the orthodoxy of belief established at Nicaea and later councils would lead to charges of heresy. The burning of books and killing of "heretics" was quite effective in removing traces of the opposing views on Christianity that flourished during the pre-Nicaea period. Only recently have scholars felt free to begin examining this period with critical scholarship.

This game attempts to examine this period using recently discovered documents and the scholarly work of people who have tried to uncover the debates that raged at this time. The game examines the alternative views of the nature of Jesus of Nazareth and the basic nature of the message he sought to bring to the world. Students should be aware that the process of reconstructing the history of this period necessarily requires conjecture and speculation. Some of this has reached popular culture in the fictional work *The DaVinci Code* by Dan Brown, which invented and distorted historical material. Possibly the most extreme position is found in *The Jesus Mysteries* by Timothy Freke and Peter Gandy. They argue that the original Christianity was a Jewish construction of a mystery cult based on those of Dionysus, Osiris, and Mithras. This idea reached popular culture in the movie *Religulous* by Bill Maher. It also receives somewhat more scholarly support in Barrie Wilson's book *How Jesus Became Christian*.

On its surface, modern Christianity appears to be very diverse. As Bart Ehrman notes in *Lost Christianities*, this runs the gamut from the snake-handling Pentecostals of Appalachia to the formal mysticism of the Greek Orthodox. However, virtually every Christian from the entire spectrum would still affirm the Nicaean Creed developed at the council that forms the basis of this game. At the beginning of the fourth century C.E., the scope of Christian belief was so broad as to be almost un-recognizable as parts of one religion. The nature of Jesus and his relationship with God, which forms the core conflict of this game, was hotly debated. It was not even clear to some Christians that the God of Jesus was the same as the God of Abraham. The two predominant positions have been labeled Alexandrian and Arian after the individuals most closely associated with them. The sections that follow explore in more detail these and other positions that emerged on the nature of Jesus.

This game places students inside a political process to establish the core beliefs that are held by virtually all modern Christians. The theological convictions of the people involved in the debates at Nicaea were sincerely and deeply felt. These people were willing to die for their beliefs. Like any meeting to resolve such a conflict, there is a political aspect to the debates. The council may produce a document that truly unifies all of Christendom but papers over some of the differences, or it may produce a specific document that can be used to marginalize and eliminate some Christians as heretics. Small changes in language, even a single letter in a word, can have a major impact on the outcome and whether a truly universal church is possible or the Church will split between competing ideas.

It is not the intention of this game to challenge or affirm Christian orthodoxy but only to show that, during the period in which it developed, there was a lively discussion and no clear consensus. Furthermore, the nature and structure of Christianity might possibly have been very different had the Council of Nicaea and subsequent councils during the fourth century come to different conclusions.

As Bart Ehrman notes in *Lost Christianities*, much of the debate about the nature of Jesus Christ had been settled by the time of the Council of Nicaea. There was an emerging "proto-orthodoxy" (to use his term) that had succeeded in marginalizing the more extreme positions of the first three centuries. However, it is also quite clear that these extreme positions still persisted as regional variations and that they had not yet been suppressed by the burning of their texts and the elimination of adherents who refused to recant their positions.

PROLOGUE—WELCOME TO THE COUNCIL OF NICAEA (NICEA)[1]

What an amazing time you live in. As a bishop of the Christian church, you have endured years of persecution. You have been imprisoned and tortured, all for your faith. Through it all, you have clung to your belief in Jesus as Savior of the world.

Now the world is suddenly Christian. Constantine has made Christianity legal and even the preferred religion of the empire. Suddenly, instead of having their property taken and being barred from public service, Christians are in demand. In fact, Constantine has made being a Christian a prerequisite for many government posts. He is building churches and returning property that was taken during the recent persecution. It is almost more than you can comprehend. You have heard some of the priests in your city compare Constantine to Christ in glowing terms and talk about the establishment of Christ's kingdom on earth. Is this the kingdom that was foretold? You think it possible that these sentiments may be a bit overblown, but the reason for the excitement is clear.

Now, at the order of Constantine himself, you have arrived in Nicaea for the first great church-wide council of bishops to be sanctioned by the state. There have been many local councils to settle matters of theology and policy but never anything on the scale of this. You have heard that 250 bishops will attend, with their presbyters as well. There must be more than 1000 people here enjoying the hospitality of the emperor.

You do have some concerns about the direction things are going. Constantine seems determined to arrive at a single statement of Christian faith. As long as that is in accord with your personal faith, it will be fine, but you worry that some of the bishops will push through ideas and statements that you will find unacceptable. If that happens, you worry that Constantine may turn on those who refuse to go along and will urge the bishops to excommunicate them or worse. Until now, the Church has been able to accommodate a wide range of interpretations of who Jesus was and what he wanted his followers to do. Some have strayed from the faith, but most have been true to the faith of the apostles. Most of the more extreme theological positions have been marginalized, and you sense a broad agreement on most issues.

You are also concerned about the recent influx of new members into the Church. Some of the people you have seen join seem to lack the deep faith of those who were members during the years of persecution. When it was unpopular to be a Christian, you could be confident that those whom you baptized really had faith. But now that membership is a prerequisite for civil service, you see more and more people coming for baptism but not living the life of a Christian. The other problem with the rush to become Christian is that many of the new converts are not interested in progressing through the deeper levels of understanding of the faith. They read the introductory tracts in circulation, such as the Gospel of Mark, and think that they know it all. They lack the commitment to learn the deeper mysteries that you want to share with all of the faithful. Is this the price of having Constantine's open support for the Church? Will the faith survive its success?

You had a long talk with Eusebius (you-SEE-bee-us) of Caesarea over lunch. He is clearly a very well educated and thoughtful person. He explained that the most important issue is the position of Arius and his followers on the relationship of Jesus to God. Eusebius explained that Arius has a strong belief that God alone is God and eternal. God existed before all time and is completely unknowable by man. Although Jesus is God's "only Begotten Son," he did not exist through all time as God did. If God begat Jesus, then the implication is that God preceded Jesus. Since God is indivisible, Jesus is not the same as God but is his issue, his Son. The Son is not the Father.

Eusebius seems to support Arius, but he was a bit vague when you asked him about the place of the Holy Spirit in the scheme of things. He seems to think the Holy Spirit is a creation of God and therefore he is not God either. There is a clear logic in this. However, the Gospel of John states very clearly that "In the beginning was the Word, and the Word was with God, and the Word was God. He was in the beginning with God." You challenged Eusebius with this, and his answer was that the Word, Jesus, was present at the beginning of the universe, and that all things that are were made through the Word. But just because Jesus was present at the beginning of time and at the beginning of the universe does not mean that Jesus existed in the same way that God does. If God created Jesus before there was time, then Jesus would have existed from the beginning of time but would still be an issue from God. The alternate view would be that Jesus was, ontologically, identical with God in being or substance. Eusebius asked your position on the issue, but you deferred and asked for more time to decide. You will need to pray about this and read the scriptures. You look forward to hearing more about this controversy.

You also had a meeting with Ossius (O-see-us), who will chair the council. He also pressed you for your opinion on the Arian "heresy," as he called it. He accused Arius of being a polytheist by setting up three different gods. His own belief is that there is only one God. Eusebius discussed this with you and argued that it would be silly for Jesus to pray to God as he does many times in the scriptures if he is in fact God. That would simply be talking to himself. You have a sense that neither side is willing to give much to find a compromise. You will need to sort this out and meditate on it before you cast your vote.

After a lavish dinner sponsored by Constantine, you found yourself with a group of followers of Valentinus (Val-en-TINE-us). They seem to take the ideas of Arius one step further. They believe Jesus was born a normal mortal man and that only when he was baptized did he receive the Word. They believe that God could never take form in a human body. Instead, God provides some souls with esoteric, saving knowledge (gnosis), and they impart it through their teaching to others. Jesus was, at best, a divine soul, temporarily inhabiting a human body, imparting saving knowledge to those able to hear and receive it. Some followers of Valentinus deny the validity of the Gospel of John altogether and would substitute the Gospel of Thomas in its place. You are not very familiar with this Gospel and will need to study it as well. The followers of Valentinus also suggested you read the Gospel of Philip. You are

very disturbed by their position. They seem to have some strange ideas about church organization as well. They elect their bishops on a rotating basis and allow women to participate in church leadership on the same basis as men. Although you see this as consistent with the apostle Paul's statements that in Christ there is no male and female and no slave and free, it does seem to violate the apostle Paul's comments about the place of women in the church. The followers of Valentinus also accuse the leaders of the Church of editing the scriptures to remove the roles of women and are particularly concerned that Mary Magdalene has been slighted. They suggest you read her Gospel as well. Finally, they tend to drop cryptic statements and ask you mathematical questions that you don't understand. They seem a bit like a cult to you, with secret handshakes or something. You sense they have secrets that they will only share within their group. This makes you uncomfortable, and you feel like a second-class Christian in their presence. But they have invited you to meet with them and to provide you with instruction if you are willing. Again, you have some reading to do and some questions to ask.

Some groups at dinner would not even sit with each other. This does not speak well for reaching accord in the council. You asked Eusebius about one group that was clearly ostracized, and he explained that they were bishops who had turned over scriptures to the Romans during the persecution. Many feel that they should not even be here. Nevertheless, Constantine has asked them to attend, and no one would think of challenging him on this. At this point, everyone is so excited to have the emperor's blessing on the council that no one will question anything he does for fear of offending him.

You sense that there may be some other issues as well. You caught snippets of conversation about eunuchs. The rumor is that one of the bishops castrated himself and now lives with a woman in his house. This is troubling. There are also some who question the idea that the bishops should even meet to decide on a basic creed for the faithful or that there should be a single statement of faith required of all Christians. Finally, you heard rumors that some of the presbyters in attendance may be guilty of persecution of other Christians. This is hard to understand. When Christians were persecuted by the empire, there was a tendency to stand together. Now that Christians are publicly favored by Constantine, it seems clear that some are trying to grab earthly power in ways that you find un-Christian. You will need to be on the lookout for these people. Apparently, there are two groups claiming to be the true church in Alexandria, followers of Alexander and followers of Meletius (meh-LEH-tee-us), and this has led to violence over church buildings and resources. Similar problems are rumored in Carthage and Antioch.

Clearly, it will be an interesting few months as these issues are raised and settled. You have only been here a few days, and already you are concerned that the council will not succeed in bringing everyone together. Frankly, the last few days have made you very uncomfortable. You will need to watch your step and do a lot of careful thought and prayer on these issues.

HOW TO PLAY THIS GAME

This is a "reacting" game. Reacting games are historical role-playing games in which students take on assigned characters to learn about moments in history. After a few preparatory lectures, the game begins and the students are in charge. Set in moments of heightened historical tension, the games place students in the roles of historical figures. By reading the gamebook and their individual role sheets, students discover their objectives, potential allies, and the forces that stand between them and victory. They must then attempt to achieve victory through formal speeches, informal debate, negotiations, and (sometimes) conspiracy. Outcomes sometimes part from actual history; a postmortem session sets the record straight.

The following is an outline of what you will encounter in this game and what you will be expected to do.

Game Setup

Your instructor will spend some time before the beginning of the game helping you to understand the historical context for the game. During the setup period, you will use several different kinds of materials:

- The gamebook (from which you are reading now) includes historical information, rules and elements of the game, and essential documents.
- Your instructor will provide you with a role sheet, which provides a short biography of the historical figure you will model in the game as well as that person's ideology, objectives, responsibilities, and resources. Your role may be an actual historical figure or a composite.

In addition to the gamebook, you may also be required to read historical documents or books written by historians. These provide additional information and arguments for use during the game.

Read all of this contextual material and all of these documents and sources before the game begins. And just as important, go back and reread these materials throughout the game. A second and third reading while *in role* will deepen your understanding and alter your perspective, for ideas take on a different aspect when seen through the eyes of a partisan actor.

Students who have carefully read the materials and who know the rules of the game will invariably do better than those who rely on general impressions and uncertain memories.

Game Play

Once the game begins, class sessions are presided over by students. In most cases, a single student serves as a kind of presiding officer. The instructor then becomes the gamemaster (GM) and takes a seat in the back of the room. Although they do not lead the class sessions, GMs may do any of the following:

- Pass notes.
- Announce important events. Some of these events are the result of student actions; others are instigated by the GM.
- Redirect proceedings that have gone off-track.

The presiding officer is expected to observe basic standards of fairness, but as a fail-safe device, this game employs the "Podium Rule," which allows a student who has not been recognized to approach the podium and wait for a chance to speak. Once at the podium, the student has the floor and must be heard.

Role sheets contain private, secret information that students are expected to guard. You are therefore advised to exercise caution when discussing your role with others. Your role sheet probably identifies likely allies, but even they may not always be trustworthy. However, keeping your own counsel, or saying nothing to anyone, is not an option. In order to achieve your objectives, you *must* speak with others. You will never muster the voting strength to prevail without allies. Collaboration and coalition building are at the heart of every game.

These discussions must lead to action, which often means proposing, debating, and passing legislation. Therefore, someone must be responsible for introducing the measure and explaining its particulars. And always remember that this game is *only a game*—resistance, attack, and betrayal are not to be taken personally, since game opponents are merely acting as their roles direct.

Some games feature strong alliances called *factions*, which are tight-knit groups with fixed objectives. All games with factions include roles called indeterminates. They operate outside of the established factions. Not all indeterminates are entirely neutral; some are biased on certain issues. If you are in a faction, cultivating indeterminates is in your interest, since they can be convinced to support your position. If you are lucky enough to have drawn the role of an indeterminate, you should be pleased; you will likely play a pivotal role in the outcome of the game.

Game Requirements

Players will practice persuasive writing, public speaking, critical thinking, teamwork, negotiation, problem solving, collaboration, adapting to changing circumstances, and working under pressure to meet deadlines. Your instructor will explain the specific requirements for your class. In general, though, this game asks you to perform the following three distinct activities.

Reading and Writing

This standard academic work is carried on more purposefully in a role-playing game, since what you read is put to immediate use, and what you write is meant to persuade others to act the way you want them to. The reading load may have slight variations from role to role; the writing requirement depends on your particular course. Papers are often policy statements, but they can also be autobiographies, battle plans, spy reports, newspapers, poems, or after-game reflections. Papers provide the foundation for the speeches delivered in class.

Public Speaking and Debate

In the course of a game, almost everyone is expected to deliver at least one formal speech from the podium (the length of the game and the size of the class will determine the number of speeches). Debate follows. Debate can be impromptu, raucous, and fast paced, and it results in decisions voted on by the body. Gamemasters may stipulate that students must deliver their papers from memory when at the podium or may insist that students wean themselves from dependency on written notes as the game progresses.

Wherever the game imaginatively puts you, it will surely not put you in the classroom of a twenty-first-century American college. Accordingly, the colloquialisms and familiarities of today's college life are out of place. Never open your speech with a salutation like "Hi guys" when something like "Fellow citizens!" would be more appropriate.

Never be friendless when standing at the podium. Do your best to have at least one supporter second your proposal, come to your defense, or admonish inattentive members of the body. Note-passing and side conversations, although common occurrences, will likely spoil the effect of your speech, so you and your supporters should insist on order before such behavior becomes too disruptive. Ask the presiding officer to assist you, if necessary, and ask the gamemaster as a last resort.

Strategizing

Communication among students is an essential feature of this game. You will find yourself writing emails, texting, attending out-of-class meetings, or gathering for meals on a fairly regular basis. The purpose of frequent communication is to lay out a strategy for advancing your agenda and thwarting the agenda of your opponents, and to hatch plots to ensnare individuals troubling to your cause. When communicating with a fellow student in or out of class, always assume that he or she is speaking to you in role. If you want to talk about the "real world," make that clear.

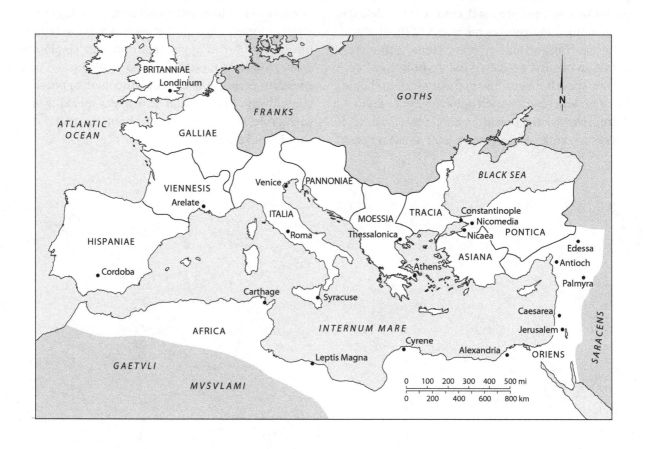

2

Historical Background

THE DEVELOPMENT OF CHRISTIANITY

The early development of the Christian religion was hampered by the fact that the active ministry of Jesus of Nazarus (or Nazareth) was limited to no more than three years and that he left no written documents. Jesus was a Jew who, if one uses only his reported words, was intent on reforming some of the practices of Judaism. There is no indication that he saw himself founding a new or separate religion. His acceptance of the role as "Son of Man," the Jewish code for Messiah, was slow and seemingly somewhat reluctant. Some of his followers clearly believed he would found an earthly kingdom that would throw off the rule of Rome and reestablish the Jewish state as an independent nation. His life and the lives of his direct disciples coincided with a period of sporadic outbursts of violence against the Roman administration in Judea, which culminated in the destruction of Jerusalem in 70 C.E.

The actual nature of the historical person of Jesus is a question that has aroused considerable scholarly and speculative activity. It is difficult to determine whether Jesus was a Jewish reformer intent on reforming Jewish practices (see, for example, Matt. 23), overthrowing the priestly control of the temple (such as the commercial use of the temple; see Luke 19:45), a revolutionary leader intent on throwing out the Roman occupiers, or a claimant to the throne of Israel occupied by the Herod family (see Luke 19:25–40 and John 12:12–15). There is no evidence in the Bible we have today that he saw himself as the founder of a global religion.

When seen from two thousand years later, most people see only the image that the Church has constructed and projected during that long period. Only in the past two centuries have the tools of modern scholarship, critical analysis of texts, and archaeological discovery begun to open up the conflicting and interesting facts about Jesus. There are excellent scholarly sources noted in the resources for the game. There are also a wide range of speculative sources in popular literature as well.

These raise questions that are impossible to answer with any certainty. Was Jesus married? Did he have children? Was his birth the product of a liaison between Mary and a Roman legionnaire named Tiberius Julius Abdes Pantera?[1] Did Jesus have supernatural powers as a child? Did Jesus really die on the cross, or was he replaced by a surrogate, possibly Simon of Cyrene?

Speculative writing about Jesus is not limited to present-day authors. Writers in the second century C.E. constructed fictional accounts of Jesus's early life, such as the Infancy Gospel of Thomas (see table 1). In the seventh century C.E., the Qur'an also contains an alternate story about Jesus's crucifixion.

> And [for] their saying, "Indeed, we have killed the Messiah, Jesus, the son of Mary, the messenger of Allah." And they did not kill him, nor did they crucify him; but [another] was made to resemble him to them. And indeed, those who differ over it are in doubt about it. They have no knowledge of it except the following of assumption. And they did not kill him, for certain.
>
> *(Qur-ān 4:157)*

For the purposes of the game, anything written about the historical Jesus can be used as a source, whether it is considered accurate by all modern scholars or not. It is known that many rumors about Jesus were in wide circulation at the time of the Council of Nicaea. It can be assumed that bishops at the council would have had some familiarity with these rumors and allegations. However, if you choose to speculate about Jesus in ways that conflict with the account in the accepted scriptures, you will risk being branded a heretic.

E. P. Sanders's *The Historical Figure of Jesus* is an excellent scholarly treatment of this topic, as are the works of John Dominic Crossan, *The Historical Jesus: The Life of a Mediterranean Jewish Peasant* and *Jesus: A Revolutionary Biography*.

Bart Ehrman's *Lost Christianities* is an excellent source for examining the controversies among early Christians about the nature of Jesus/Christ. The full spectrum of major opinions among Christian groups is well described in this work, along with the tactics they used to make their cases, primarily through the use and abuse of texts. Another book by Ehrman, *Jesus—Apocalyptic Prophet of the New Millennium*, is another treatment of the historical Jesus.

After Jesus's death around 30 C.E., his followers struggled to redefine their roles in light of the reality of his death. They reported profound experiences of his continuing presence. These were so real that they could account for them only on the assumption that he had been raised from the dead. This apparently came as a surprise to them, and only the female followers are reported to have understood it at first (see Matt. 28:1–10). The idea that Jesus had to die to redeem the sins of all humankind was a theology that did not develop until after the Council of Nicaea.

The early church described in the New Testament was essentially Jewish in all respects. James the Just, Jesus's brother (Gal. 1:20), was a revered ascetic and Jewish leader in Jerusalem. He inherited the mantle of Jesus, and the Gospel of Thomas quotes Jesus as saying James is superior to him. The Gospel of Thomas attributes the kind of mystical importance to James that the Gospel of John attributes to Jesus. This may be why the Gospel of Thomas, considered a Gnostic (NOS-tik) text, was eventually rejected from the emerging canon of the Church: to diminish James and enhance the role of the apostle Peter and the theology of the apostle Paul, which runs directly counter to the writings of James.

It is almost shocking that there is *no single historical reference to Jesus by anyone from the Jewish or Christian faiths until the second century*. This is doubly shocking given the detailed records and writings of Roman officials of the time. More nonbiblical documents provide historical evidence for James the Just and John the Baptist than for Jesus. The only non-Christian references to Jesus in all of the existing literature of the first century C.E.

are two brief paragraphs found in Josephus's *Antiquities of the Jews*. One only identifies Jesus as the brother of James. The other, more detailed reference (*Antiquities* 18.3.3, Loeb 18.63–64) contains language that is almost certainly not original to Josephus. Ehrman and others have suggested that even the first reference is an addition by later Christian scribes (Ehrman 1999, pp. 60–63).

Josephus was a Jewish general who surrendered to the Romans after the defeat of his forces in Galilee. He appears to have convinced most of his soldiers to commit suicide and then decided to surrender himself. He then became a Roman sympathizer. Like all histories, Josephus's work reflects his personal bias and may have been subject to later editing by the Christian scribes who preserved his works. (The notion of bias simply means that the author does not write from a completely objective, impersonal perspective. Bias does not mean that the account is false, only that the writer has a personal investment in the issues he discusses.)

The biblical accounts of both the life of Jesus and the subsequent actions of his disciples are contained in the collection of writings we call the New Testament, most notably in the four Gospels (these are attributed to Matthew, Mark, Luke, and John, but the actual authors are unknown) and the Acts of the Apostles. The latter document was written by the same author as the Gospel of Luke, and it is the only one of many written accounts of the postresurrection period that was included in the New Testament.

The other major source for this period that will be used in the game is *The History of the Church* by Eusebius of Caesarea, who appears as a character in this game. Eusebius was a bishop from Caesarea in Palestine. He was a scholar and had access to one of the finest libraries of Christian documents in existence. Thus, his writing is filled with quotations from other sources. In some cases, the quotations he gives are the only existing remnants of these texts. Eusebius was convinced that the arrival of Constantine as the single emperor of the Roman Empire represented the beginning of the Kingdom of God on earth. He treats Constantine as a messianic figure and writes glowingly of him. Although Eusebius was generally a member of the proto-orthodox establishment, he was also a participant in the Arian heresy and came to Nicaea under conditional excommunication for his reported support of Arius. One reason that his writings have been preserved is that they support the orthodox position of the Church as it emerged from the Council of Nicaea. As with Josephus, it is impossible to identify editorial changes that might have been made in copying his works.

THE FIRST CENTURY

The "official story" of early Christianity that follows relies on the New Testament and on Eusebius. Students are cautioned that both sources reflect the established orthodoxy that developed in the fourth century and are therefore potentially unreliable as a full, complete, and accurate rendering of actual history.

The First Crisis—The Council of Jerusalem

The first major crisis reported in the Acts of the Apostles was the decision on how to include Gentiles in the Jesus movement. James and the leaders in Jerusalem wanted everyone to accept the Torah law and follow the dietary and ritual laws of Moses. They also believed Gentile converts should be circumcised, as were all Jewish males. This was obviously an obstacle to Gentile converts, and Jesus's own words seemed to downplay the importance of following Torah slavishly without understanding its divine intent. In this sense, Jesus replicates the position taken by other rabbis of his time. We know from recent archaeological findings at Aphrodesia (near the modern southwestern Turkish village of Geyre) that Jewish synagogues around the Mediterranean had attracted a large following of Gentiles who were attracted to the monotheistic beliefs of the Jews but who were unwilling to submit to circumcision and the Jewish dietary laws. In the most well-documented example, fully 43 percent of the

Sadducees and Pharisees

donors listed for a building project were specifically non-Jewish people who participated in the life of the synagogue and contributed to its construction (Crossan and Reed 2004, p. 24). This sort of non-Jewish worshiper may be "those among you who fear God" referred to in Acts 13:16.

The apostle Paul was a Jewish convert to Christianity. According to Acts, he traveled around Asia Minor, converting Gentiles to Christianity. Crossan and Reed (2004, p. xi) have suggested that the most receptive audience for Paul would have been among Gentiles in Jewish synagogues, sometimes called the "God Fearers." Paul did not believe these converts needed to be circumcised, and this set up a direct conflict with James the Just. Acts 15 reports that Paul came to meet with James and the Council of Jerusalem to work out a solution. In the end, James ruled that Gentiles should not be troubled with observing this part of the law, but they should "abstain from the pollutions of idols and from unchastity and from what is strangled and from blood" (Acts 15:20 and Gal. 2:1–10).

The preceding description is the canonical view of these events based on the scriptures. Some (for example, Pagels, *The Gnostic Gospels* and *The Gnostic Paul*) have suggested that the apostle Paul was a Gnostic and that some of the events recorded in the book of Acts were constructed later to show that Paul considered himself subject to the twelve apostles and to give credibility to the bishops who traced their ancestry to the apostles in their efforts to control the Gnostic Christians. (Most scholars might admit a trace of Gnosticism in the writings of the apostle Paul but would reject the assertion that he was a Gnostic in the full sense.)

The Second Crisis—
The Destruction of Jerusalem

The period from 60 C.E. to 70 C.E. was one of considerable conflict both because of political intrigue by the rulers and conflict between different religious factions. Sanders argues that the revolt against the Romans occurred suddenly and had its roots in the actions of the procurator Florus, who took money

from the temple. There had been substantial resistance to any Roman actions that violated the Jewish religious institutions (Sanders 1992, pp. 40–44). The war against the Romans started in 66 C.E. It ended when the Romans surrounded Jerusalem in 70 C.E. They took it and killed everyone they could. Reports by Josephus say that blood ran in the streets. The sack of Jerusalem probably led to the death of many Jewish followers of Jesus and discredited the center of the movement.

Shortly before the revolt began, James the Just, Jesus's brother, was killed on the order of the high priest. The mantle of leadership of the Jesus movement passed first to Clophas, Jesus's uncle, and brother of Joseph, according to Eusebius. After Clophas, Eusebius reports that Simeon, the son of Clophas, and Jesus's cousin, became head of the church in Jerusalem and moved the leadership out of Jerusalem before the Bar Kokhba revolt in 132 C.E.

After the destruction of Jerusalem in 70 C.E., what remained of the Church were Jewish Christians and the Gentile Christians living outside of Jerusalem. The growth of the movement meant that Gentile Christians quickly began to outnumber the Jewish followers. The center of gravity of what would become Christianity shifted from its Jewish base to the Gentile converts. Within a generation, arguments broke out between members of the Jesus movement and Jews who rejected his teachings.

In addition to arguments between Jews and Christians, there were debates within the Church. The early church also espoused a radical equality, which some modern scholars believe led to the exercise of power in the Church by slaves and women. There is clear evidence that women participated in the Church at all levels during this period, but this ended as ecclesiastical power became increasingly concentrated in the hands of male bishops alone. It has also been argued (Stephenson 2009, pp. 38–41) that the Church's protection of women and orphans and the ban on abortion for Christians contributed to rapid growth of the Christian population at a time when infanticide and abortion were common among the general population.

Not long after Jesus's death, the Roman Empire began to persecute Christians. This persecution was sporadic rather than constant. Jesus had been executed by Rome, perhaps for advocating a message that threatened its supremacy. Jesus had said, "Verily I say unto you, there be some standing here, which shall not taste of death, till they see the Son of man coming in his kingdom" (Matt. 16:28). Among the earliest Christians, there was a clear expectation of the immediate return of Jesus in power to overturn the Roman Empire. But the Christians were persecuted primarily for their refusal to worship the emperor and for bringing disorder to the empire. The apostle Paul was arrested in Jerusalem and was sent to Rome, where he was finally executed. Christians were killed wholesale in the Coliseum and elsewhere. They were a perfect scapegoat for Roman emperors. Martyrdom became the hallmark of faith, and many embraced it as a way to move from the oppression of Rome to a heavenly Kingdom of God. (Modern readers should consider the quest for martyrdom by a few radicalized Muslim men and women who have been led to believe they will immediately be happy in Heaven. The difference was that Christians sought to be martyred by the Roman Empire for simply professing their faith and without any violence on their part. Another useful parallel is with U.S. Muslims who continue to demonstrate their faith identity after 9/11 even though some were killed and many were blatantly persecuted—and still are—for their faith by Christian Americans.)

THE SECOND CENTURY

The second century C.E. provides documents by both Christian and pagan writers that address Christianity's growing visibility in the Roman Empire. Clement, bishop of Rome, wrote several works that were highly influential. Ignatius and Polycarp were two Christian martyrs who left extensive writings.

Pagan leaders such as Pliny the Younger and Emperor Trajan discussed how to deal with Christians. Pliny the Younger was a regional governor in what is now northern Turkey. He wrote to Trajan asking how to deal with Christians. The advice was that it was fine to punish them if they refused to make the required civic activities of worship. However, Trajan recommended that they not be actively pursued. Furthermore, Trajan advised that anonymous accusations should be ignored.

Among the many martyrs of the second century C.E., two stand out because their writings were preserved. Ignatius was a bishop in Antioch and was martyred sometime between 98 and 117 C.E. He was offered the chance to escape death, but possibly because he was an old man, he chose to embrace his fate. He was taken to Rome to be part of a spectacular death. Along the way, he wrote a number of letters to churches. These letters have been preserved and provide some insight into the issues facing the local churches. Polycarp was a bishop in Smyrna who was martyred about 50 years after Ignatius, in 155 C.E. The *Martyrdom of Polycarp* is a detailed account of his martyrdom. Apparently, Ignatius advised the young Polycarp to hide and avoid martyrdom, but in his eighties, Polycarp embraced it. At the same time, Christians were advised that martyrdom was something that God chose for them and that people should not seek it out. The writings of Ignatius, Polycarp, and others showed martyrdom as a noble calling.

The Christian response to persecution was to be model citizens of the empire. Some even wrote letters to the emperors challenging their persecution by claiming that they paid their taxes fairly and without complaint and lived model lives in every respect except for their refusal to make sacrifices to the gods. Tertullian, an African convert to Christianity who was moved to his faith by watching the deaths of martyrs, noted, "we hold everything in common but our spouses," whereas "most people shared nothing else" (Pagels, *The Gnostic Gospels*, pp. 50–51). Although these arguments got them nowhere with the emperors, who clearly understood the subversive nature of the Christian message of equality and its threat to the supremacy of human powers, it did have an impact on the society as a whole.

Christians were not the only major religious group persecuted by the Romans. The followers of Mithras were also suppressed when they began to grow too large and powerful. The empire had assimilated a large number of areas with local religions and gods. It tolerated most of them and asked only that citizens observe the feasts and make occasional sacrifices to the Roman gods. As long as people did that, they were free to worship otherwise as they wished. Jews were exempted from these sacrifices, which were not permitted in their faith. The Romans appear to have tolerated Jewish practices because of the antiquity of the Jewish people or because the father of Herod the Great had helped Julius Caesar capture Egypt. Caesar issued edicts recognizing Jewish rights (Josephus, *Antiquities of the Jews* XIV 8), which were continued by the Senate after his death (Josephus, *Antiquities of the Jews* XIV 10.22).

Christians, on the other hand, had a more exclusive or exceptional view of their own religious practices compared with the non-Christian citizens of the empire, who they would have described as pagan. Christians believed that Jesus was the only way to salvation and that their God was the only true God. Therefore, they refused to observe the Roman sacrificial practices because to do so would be a form of idolatry. As a result, they were often blamed for anything that went wrong in society. If the crops failed or there was a flood, earthquake, or military defeat, it must be because the Christians refused to make sacrifices and had angered the gods, who were taking vengeance.

The second century saw the emergence of many variations of Christian belief. Gnosticism emerged among followers of Valentinus (c.100–c.160 C.E.). Marcion founded another variation on Christianity around 144 C.E. in Rome. The details of their beliefs will be discussed later. These variations of Chris-

tian belief attracted significant attention and opposition.

The Church, faced with a wide and often contradictory range of beliefs about Jesus and the theology of Christianity, used creeds as a weapon against heretics. These statements of belief could be tailored to support the view of the writer and demonstrate the ways in which the "heretics" were failing to follow the true way of Christ. The creeds that remain today are those that supported what became the orthodox position in the fourth century C.E. and beyond. One can assume that Gnostics and Marcionites may have had creeds as well, but they are lost today because they were considered heretical by the post-Nicaea Church.

The Apostles' Creed was possibly an early effort to form a statement of Christian belief that would marginalize the more extreme positions (Gonzalez 1984, pp. 63–64). This presumably grew out of the questions asked of people preparing for baptism. This creed dates to at least as early as the middle of the second century C.E. Whether they accepted it or not, all at Nicaea would be presumed to know this creed, which reads as follows:

I believe in God the Father almighty.

I believe in Jesus Christ, the Son of God, who was born of the Holy Ghost and of Mary the virgin, was crucified under Pontius Pilate, and died, and rose on the third day, and ascended into heaven and sits at the right of the Father, and will come to judge the living and the dead.

I believe in the Holy Ghost, the holy church, and the resurrection of the flesh.

This creed would not be acceptable to anyone who believed that Jesus did not actually die on the cross, as was the case for some Gnostics. But, in general, this statement of faith, still in use today, is rather nonspecific on the issues facing the Council of Nicaea.

Another creed was written by Irenaeus, bishop of Lyon, in the late second century (MacCulloch 2010, pp. 129–30). This creed would also be impossible for a Gnostic or Marcionite to accept, and it reads as follows:

> God the Father, uncreated, beyond grasp, invisible, one God the maker of all; this is the first and foremost article of our faith. But the second article is the Word of God, the Son of God, Christ Jesus our Lord, who was shown forth by the prophets according to the design of their prophecy and according to the manner in which the Father disposed; and through Him were made all things whatsoever. He also, in the end of times . . . became a man among men, visible and tangible, in order to abolish death and bring to light life, and bring about the communion of God and man. And the third article is the Holy Spirit, through whom the prophets prophesied and the patriarchs were taught about God . . . and who in the end of times has been poured forth in a new manner upon humanity over all the earth, renewing man to God.

Gnostics and Marcionites would not accept that the ultimate God was maker of the world. They would also have difficulty with a tangible Jesus or the Holy Spirit speaking through the prophets and teaching the patriarchs.

Another response to the challenge of the Gnostics and Marcionites was the development of literature to defend the orthodox position. The Gnostics and Marcionites may have had similar literature, but, if so, it is lost. After the Council of Nicaea, documents that did not support the mainstream view were destroyed or not copied and thereby preserved.

Around the end of the second century C.E., Irenaeus began to develop a theology of Jesus as the new Adam. His idea was that God's purpose from the beginning was to reconcile people to himself, and that Jesus was the vehicle that made this possible through his death and resurrection.

The transition from the second to the third century saw major thinkers in the mainstream turn their attention to defining a Christian theology. Clement of Alexandria, Tertullian of Carthage, and Origen of Alexandria all contributed to the development of the growing understanding of what would become the mainstream of Christian thought. Tertullian wrote scathing attacks on heretics. Both Clement and Origen added elements of Platonic philosophy to the understanding of God and his relationship to Jesus.

THE THIRD CENTURY

The third century opened with significant developments in the diversity of the theology of the Church. In Alexandria, the young Origen began studying the many manuscripts of both the Jewish and Christian writings. He assembled a document that included several versions of the Jewish texts in both Hebrew and Greek. He did the same with multiple copies of the four Gospels.

Origen's education was rich in Platonic philosophy, and he viewed the scriptures through a Greek lens. He understood the creation story in Genesis as a story containing rich spiritual insights but not as literal history. In the same way, the Gospels were meant to teach the truths of God but not to relay every single historical detail of the life of Jesus. Origen's understanding of the scriptures stood in sharp contrast with that of Christians in Syria, including Antioch. There, the scriptures were viewed literally as historical accounts.

Origen eventually got in trouble with Demetrius, bishop of Alexandria. He had begun preaching in churches, and when challenged with the fact that he was not ordained, he convinced a group of local clergy to ordain him. Ultimately, he was forced to leave Alexandria, and he took up residence in Caesarea.

The theology that Origen developed also contained several elements that led to his exile from Alexandria. Most importantly, Origen saw the Word, Jesus, as subordinate to God the Father, and the Holy Spirit as subordinate to the Word. The technical term for this position was subordinationism, and it was considered a heresy by the mainstream church leadership.

Origen also wrote about wisdom (in Greek, *gnosis*) as part of what Jesus brought to the world. Although Origen did not subscribe to Gnostic cosmology, this was enough to associate him with the Gnostics. As a result, many of his writings have been lost. However, his work made a formidable contribution to Christian orthodoxy. His library of manuscripts passed to Pamphilus, a priest and teacher in Caesarea who taught Eusebius of Caesarea, who was a major figure at the Council of Nicaea. Given this lineage, it is no wonder that Eusebius was willing to provide a home to Arius when he was driven from Alexandria.

At the same time that Origen was writing in Alexandria and later in Caesarea, Paul of Samosata was creating a controversy in Antioch. Paul of Samosata was bishop of Antioch from 260 C.E. until he was removed by a synod of bishops in 268 C.E. Eusebius of Caesarea records the charges against him in book VII, chapter 30, of his *History of the Church*. Paul of Samosata believed that Jesus was born a normal man and was then adopted as God's Son. This belief is known as adoptionism and as monarchianism. Paul of Samosata believed that although Jesus was initially a mere man, through his adoption by God and his receipt of the Word of God, he became totally one with God. This was one solution to the question of how Jesus could be both man and God, and it was the opposite of the more mainstream position that God became man in Jesus.

Lucian of Antioch was an associate of Paul of Samosata and founded a school at which several people attending the Council of Nicaea studied. His pupils included Arius and Eusebius of Nicomedia.

Another controversy in the third-century Church grew out of the response of Christians to persecution. Persecution of Christians was not constant, and it tended to be more intense during times of relative peace. When the authorities were distracted by wars, they had little energy to persecute Christians. The first empire-wide persecution of Christians was instituted by Emperor Decius around 249 C.E. Decius issued an edict that re-quired everyone to make sacrifices to the gods and burn incense to Decius. Since Julius Caesar, emperors had been worshiped as gods, and Decius wanted to restore the old ways as a way to restore the stability of the empire that was associated with this practice. This presented a new challenge to Christians, who could not perform these required rituals.

The reason for the general persecution of Christians may be that their numbers and wealth had grown to the point that they were a visible presence in many places. Churches had been built, and people worshiped openly.

The result of the decree of Decius led to a new challenge within the Church that divided Christians and led to issues that the Council of Nicaea would need to resolve 75 years later. Christians had several responses to the challenge of the decree of Decius. Some refused to perform the rituals and took the name "confessors." These Christians were often punished but were not always martyred, so they returned to their local churches, holding their refusal as a badge of honor. Christians who offered the required sacrifices were in many places branded "apostates" by the confessors.

The division between confessors and apostates led to major divisions in the Church. Nowhere was this clearer than in Carthage (modern Libya). Cyprian was the bishop of Carthage at the beginning of the persecution. He fled to avoid the issue, and when he returned, he believed that Christians who made the required sacrifices should be forgiven and welcomed back into the Church. There is certainly a scriptural basis for forgiveness, and Cyprian had plenty of reasons for his approach.

On the other side of the issue were the Novatianists (no-VAH-tee-an-ists). Novatian lived in Rome during the persecution of Decius. The persecution was so intense that for a short period it was impossible to elect a new leader (pope) for the Roman church. When an election was held, Novatian lost to Cornelius and proved a sore loser. He found a group of bishops who agreed to consecrate him as pope, and he proceeded to try to take over from

Cornelius. Novatian sent out apostles and tried to take control of the Church in various areas. The main issue for Novatian seems to have been that the apostate should not be allowed back into the Church.

The followers of Novatian were most successful in Carthage, where they founded a separate church that existed in parallel with the church recognized by Rome and Alexandria. One of the issues that would plague Constantine 50 years later was how to resolve the conflict between the two churches that emerged in Carthage. The major issue dividing them was how to deal with apostates. The Novatianists did not accept the idea that the Church could grant forgiveness to the apostates, and they wanted the apostates permanently eliminated from the Church.

The persecution of Decius lasted until 260 C.E., when Gallienus became emperor. His edict that Christians be tolerated led to 40 years of coexistence.

THE FOURTH CENTURY—THE MOVE INTO THE MAINSTREAM

In 303 C.E., Diocletian began what is often called the "Great" Persecution. This was the harshest and most widespread attack on Christians in the empire. Several edicts were issued by the four emperors controlling the western and eastern parts of the empire. Diocletian and Galerius in the eastern region were most vigorous in confiscating property and requiring that Christians sacrifice to the Roman gods. They also removed Christians and some others from the army. Constantius in Britain and Gaul was least vigorous in following through with the persecution but still confiscated some Church property. It is thought that Constantius had members of his household who were Christian and that this could have led him to be more tolerant.

When Constantine became emperor in 306 C.E., he returned confiscated property and ended the persecution. That same year, Maxentius took control of Italy and issued an edict of toleration there. The persecution continued in the eastern empire for at least another five years.

The reasons why Constantine ended the persecution have been debated. Constantine had seen the high moral behavior of the Christians, which probably included some members of his own family. When Constantine embraced Christianity and then chose to make it his preferred religion, he did so in part in the hope that he could get everyone to behave as well as the Christians. The Edict of Milan, issued in 313 by Constantine and Licinius, allowed Christians to worship openly and returned property confiscated in earlier persecutions throughout the empire. For the first time, Christianity became fully recognized.

It is not clear that Constantine had a clear understanding of Christianity at this time or understood its theology. He apparently equated the Christian God with the Supreme God and didn't want to do anything to anger the Christian God. In a sense, this is the reverse of the reasons Christians had been persecuted previously. The rulers felt Christians' failure to provide the proper sacrifices would anger the gods and cause famine or other problems. Constantine had concluded that the Christian divinity was the most powerful and important god.

With everyone now permitted to follow any religion in the empire, Constantine began to support Christian churches with money. Shortly after this, Constantine wrote a letter to Caecilianus, the bishop of Carthage, in which he wrote:

It has pleased us to contribute towards the necessary expenses of certain servants of the legitimate and most holy all-embracing religion. (Kousoulas 1997, pp. 291–92)

In another letter, he wrote to Anulinus, the proconsul in Africa, instructing him that:

It is our wish that those who live in the province entrusted to you and who are members of the all-embracing Church presided over by

Caecilianus and . . . are called clerics as is their custom, be relieved of all public functions once and for all. . . . Thus, since they offer the highest adoration to the Divinity, it seems to me that they ought to receive the highest rewards the State can offer. (Kousoulas 1997, pp. 293–94)

He allowed bishops to handle certain official acts such as freeing slaves. Being a Christian was suddenly popular and began to attract more members from the ruling class. It had always been the case that patronizing the favorite cult of the emperor was a way to gain imperial favor. Now Christianity was the favorite cult. Christianity had now become the most important religion in the empire.

It is clear that people noticed the new status given the Church and that its popularity increased rapidly. The Church, which began as a haven for the lower classes, began to attract the wealthy and powerful. Constantine began to give preference to Christians in appointments to government and military positions. In a short time, the Church went from possibly 3 percent to 5 percent of the population to possibly as much as half. Today, we would call this the problem of uncontrolled growth.

How does one preserve the core values in this situation, and what core values should be preserved? Remember that the Church's growth happened in a setting where many people practiced the Roman religion to the extent of making a few sacrifices a year. One can safely assume that many of the converts viewed Christianity in the same light. They would attend the proper feasts and make the proper sacrifices and then go about their business. The Church's answer was to begin to codify the moral standards that Christians had practiced out of faith and turn them into rules.

Another problem for the Church as it became more structured was the role of women. There is evidence that women played a prominent role in the early church into the second century C.E. When women did exercise leadership in the earliest Christian communities, they were transgressing gender boundaries that prevailed for the most part throughout the rest of the Greco-Roman world. Some of their contributions were edited out by later writers, who changed at least one name from Junia to Junias to disguise the gender of the person and minimize the role of women (Rom. 16:7). Therefore, we will probably never know the full details of women's roles and authority in the first- and second-century Church.

We do know that there were numerous female martyrs and that they were as eloquent as the men in defending the faith. Much of the appeal of Christianity in the first century of the Common Era was to the marginalized and powerless. Women and slaves were attracted by the chance for equality, at least within the community of the Church. Women may also have been attracted by the Church's moral values, which helped them avoid exploitation and abuse. The poor, widows, and elderly were attracted by the charity offered by the Church. The book of Acts reports that in some of the Christian communities in the first few centuries, all goods were held in common and distributed to everyone in need (Acts 4:32–35).

As Christians began to organize themselves into a structure or institution, they took as their models the organization of the Roman Empire. By the early second century C.E., women began to lose their social equality within the Church, and, by the time of the Council of Nicaea, all the leaders of the Church appear to have been male. Much of the early egalitarianism disappeared as hierarchical structures based on the social order of the time developed and resources grew. Christianity's emerging views on the role of women came to coincide with the prevailing cultural views of the time.

The Donatist Movement

One additional result of the Great Persecution was a split in the Church over what to do about Christians who had succumbed to persecution in some way. Some may have handed over scriptures; others may have actually made sacrifices to the Roman gods to avoid martyrdom or imprisonment.

Donatists had much in common with the Novatianists of the previous century, but they also developed an important theological difference as well. Donatists believed that the sacraments of the Church depended in some way on the religious purity of the person who performed them. Stated another way, if the priest or bishop had succumbed to persecution, his actions as a clergyman were invalid. A church commission in Rome branded the Donatists' beliefs as heresy. Their reasoning was that it was impossible to know the heart of anyone and that it was therefore impossible to be confident of your baptism and hence your salvation within the Donatists' ideology. The mainstream Church believed that baptism, for example, was an action by God, not by the priest who presided at the time.

The End of Martyrdom → Asceticism → Monasticism

For more than 200 years, martyrdom had been the highest calling of the faithful. Although Christians were not encouraged to seek martyrdom, once they were faced with it, they were expected to embrace it bravely. With the Church now accepted by the imperial powers, martyrdom was no longer an option. How could Christians demonstrate their faith? How could the Church distinguish true believers from those who join because it is popular?

The alternative to martyrdom was already being explored by groups in Egypt and elsewhere. Ascetic communities where people lived in poverty and celibacy were growing. The ability to abstain from pleasures of the flesh came to be seen as a sign of devotion to God. Monastic communities in isolated areas were also free from regular contact with other Christians and thus often developed their own specific theological understandings. The most famous of the early ascetics was Antony the Great (251–356 C.E.), who after his death became the subject of an important book on the monastic life by Athanasius.

One of the more extreme groups possibly present at the Council of Nicaea were the Gnostics, many of whom followed Valentinus, who had founded a monastic group in Egypt. It is not clear to what extent the Gnostic theology was represented officially, but the persistence of Gnostic beliefs for several more centuries argues that the Gnostics may have played at least a minor role in the minds of some of the bishops present at the council.

THE RISE OF CHURCH ORGANIZATION

It is not entirely clear when bishops (in Greek, *episcopoi*) began to appear in the earliest Christian communities. By the early second century, their office was being distinguished from those of priests (or presbyters) and deacons. The bishops were the leaders of the local church community. The presbyters were there to help the bishops and often were elevated to bishop when a vacancy occurred. The deacons were more involved with the logistics and finances than with the spiritual activities of the Church. They helped prepare Communion and were often responsible for distributing money to widows. Although deacons were not normally involved in the spiritual aspects of the Church, they apparently did sometimes rise to the position of bishop.

To understand the role of the early bishops in the Church, we need to appreciate that there was no fixed way in which they were selected and how they administered their "sees," or dioceses. The earliest bishops emerged as leaders of local Christian communities, most of which were organized around towns. These towns were usually small enough that the bishop was known by the entire population of his community. The bishop's selection was based both on his charismatic or spiritual qualities and on his abilities as an administrator. Spiritually, he was modeled on Jesus as the good shepherd of his flock. However, being a good shepherd required a talent for keeping the flock in line. The bishops primarily acted as teachers to ensure that everyone understood the orthodox position and that any inclination to deviate from it was discouraged.

It seems that most of the earliest bishops were elected by the people over whom they would have oversight (the word "episcopal" means oversight).

Regarding the ordination of bishops, Hippolytus (170–236 C.E.) says that with the agreement of all (the people), let the (other) bishops lay hands on him, and the presbyters stand in silence (from Hippolytus, *The Apostolic Tradition*, chapter 2). Ideally, a consecration was by seven bishops, but it required no fewer than three.

Later (in the fourth century), the clergy elected bishops, with ratification of their decisions being made by the laity. Later still, the bishops alone elected other bishops, with the approval of the secular magistrates. Some bishoprics were seen as hereditary, though this practice was never universally accepted.

One of the most basic responsibilities of the bishop was to represent the decisions of the synod (a gathering of bishops) to his people and to represent his people before the synod.

Although churches were generally regarded as autonomous, and each had all the essentials of a universal church, it was expected that no bishop should be a law unto himself. Churches constituted a mutual check on each other: the election of a bad bishop or the overthrow of a bishop by a church would cast a negative light on the universality of the Church and was therefore discouraged.

There was from the beginning a continuing struggle over the priority of the metropolitan (the bishop in a large urban area or city) over the diocesan bishops in smaller but adjacent areas. The early church was leery of having two bishops in the same territory. The authority of the bishop was defined as essentially territorial. This was partly to reflect the way in which secular authority operated and partly because the fight against heresy was best carried on if there were no competing bishops in the same area possibly sending conflicting signals about how best to handle heresy. Initially, all the dioceses in Christendom were considered equal in principle, but Rome eventually came to be accorded a higher status than the others.

Rome was the site of martyrdom for the apostles Peter and Paul. The apostle Paul, being a Roman citizen, was beheaded. The apostle Peter is re-ported to have been crucified, but he requested that he be crucified upside down so that his death would be less dignified than that of Jesus. These details are part of Christian lore, though the original documents that detail them have been lost (MacCulloch 2010, p. 129). The apostle Peter is revered today as the first bishop of Rome, and his tomb is in the center of St. Peter's Cathedral in the Vatican. During the early centuries of the Church, the two apostles appear together in Christian art and appear to have been revered as equals. Only later did Peter come to predominate.

The church in Rome used Jesus's statement "on this rock I will build my church" (Matt. 16:18) (a play on the word "petrus," meaning rock) as justification for the preeminent role of the apostle Peter. The Roman church came to interpret this to mean that the church in Rome would have primacy of authority over all other bishops and their dioceses.

Bishops had a variety of general responsibilities and obligations. They had the power to ordain priests and to confirm persons in the mature acceptance of their faith. A bishop was expected to teach and defend the faith, especially against heresies; to provide hospitality; to use his portion of church offerings (roughly one-quarter) to support the poor; on his birthday to give a dinner for the poor; to be the trustee for children made wards of the Church; to arbitrate lawsuits (that might otherwise have gone to secular courts, though amicable resolution was always the first priority); to provide asylum; to intercede with the secular authorities on behalf of members of their flock; to serve as ambassadors between warring factions; and to pray for the emperor and his armies (Chadwick 1979).

CHRISTOLOGY—WHAT DO CHRISTIANS BELIEVE?

Diversity at the Beginning

The four Gospels provide the central elements in the life of Jesus, and although they do contain, implicitly, various theological foundations of the meaning of Jesus for Christians, the earliest Christian theology was articulated by the apostle Paul. Christians' understanding of the meaning of Jesus did not develop in a vacuum. People used the prevailing themes and ideology of their time to explain what this new religion meant. As a result, it is easy to find elements of neo-Platonic thought and those of pagan practices in Christianity. The apostle Paul's theology was grounded in Judaism, the religion in which he was raised. However, it contains elements that resemble some aspects of the other mystery religions that were popular at the time, those of Dionysus, Mithras, and Isis/Horus.

From the very beginning, there were differences in how Christians understood Jesus and the Christian religion. The conflict between the apostle Paul and the Jewish leadership under the James the Just has already been noted. Paul, who says Christians are not bound by the Torah, stands in clear opposition to Jesus's admonition that he would not change any aspect of the Torah law (Matt. 5:19). Paul's followers would interpret the passage as meaning that Jesus would not change the "heart" of the Torah but rather the legalist rules that had developed. Jesus demonstrated this when he healed the sick on the Sabbath (Luke 6:6). Nevertheless, the issue of circumcision of Gentile Christians was a significant issue between the apostle Paul and the Jewish leadership in Jerusalem.

We know from Paul's letters that there were other teachers in competition with him. Apollos, a Jewish Christian from Alexandria, is mentioned several times:

Acts 18:24 And a certain Jew named Apollos, born at Alexandria, an eloquent man, and mighty in the scriptures, came to Ephesus.

Acts 19:1 And it came to pass, that, while Apollos was at Corinth, Paul having passed through the upper coasts came to Ephesus: and finding certain disciples, he said to them, "Did you receive the Holy Spirit when you believed?"

1 Corinthians 1:12 Now this I say, that every one of you saith, I am of Paul; and I of Apollos; and I of Cephas; and I of Christ.

1 Corinthians 3:4 For while one saith, I am of Paul; and another, I am of Apollos; are ye not carnal?

1 Corinthians 3:5 Who then is Paul, and who is Apollos, but ministers by whom ye believed, even as the Lord gave to every man?

Cephas (the apostle Peter) also traveled and preached a different message than the apostle Paul:

Galatians 2:11 When Cephas came to Antioch I opposed him to his face.

Galatians 3:1 You foolish Galatians! Who has bewitched you?

The apostle Paul also argues against "super-apostles":

2 Corinthians 11:4–5 For if someone comes to you and preaches a Jesus other than the Jesus we preached, or if you receive a different spirit from the one you received, or a different gospel from the one you accepted, you put up with it easily enough. But I do not think I am in the least inferior to those "superapostles."

We have no record of Apollos's theological contributions or how they compared with those of the apostle Paul.

The challenge of interpreting the nature of Jesus grew out of two extreme positions. On the one hand, the Jewish followers of Jesus knew him as a man, but, on the other hand, he clearly had some special connection with God. The problem with Jesus being a man and only a man was to make sense of his death. Bishop Melito of Sardis (c.170 C.E.) (http://www.kerux.com/doc/0401A1.asp; Chadwick 1979, p. 85) had already begun to develop the idea that the death of Jesus was a way to remove from all people sin that was present since the original sin of Adam and Eve in the Garden of Eden. This was analogous to the Jewish Yom Kippur Avodah service of atonement (Lev. 16:1–34), when a goat was sacrificed to atone for the sins of the people. The term "scapegoat" is derived from this ritual. Jesus's death at Passover clearly brought to mind the sacrifice of the Paschal Lamb at Passover that caused the Angel of Death to "pass over" the homes with the blood of the lamb on their doorposts and spare the firstborn males of these households from death. Jesus had to be special and different from other men for his death to accomplish this.

The alternate extreme was that Jesus was actually God in disguise. This position held that Jesus was in fact purely God and not human at all. This interpretation also leads to various problems. How could the eternal and immutable God die on the cross? Moreover, if Jesus was divine, was he different from the God of creation and of the Jews? If so, was Christianity a polytheistic religion? This would have been very upsetting to Jewish Christians. Moreover, if Jesus was purely God, then how could his life serve as an example for humans to follow?

The Church had already developed a language to discuss wrong doctrines, called heresies. Tertullian (c.160–225 C.E.) wrote a major treatise on the topic, called *Prescription against Heretics*.[2] He viewed heresy as a necessary and important test of faith, with those of weak faith falling into heresy. The true faith for Tertullian, and for those at the Council of Nicaea as well, was the faith transmitted by the apostles. Heretics are those who refuse to surrender themselves to the divine authority of God and selfishly apply pagan ideas instead. Tertullian also argued that heretics should be warned (Tit. 3:10) and then shunned rather than argued with.[3] The emerging sects of Christianity covered the entire range from Jesus as God to Jesus as man. Everyone called the positions of their opponents heresy. A common position or formulation, developing by the time of the Council of

Nicaea in 325 C.E., was essentially the midpoint between the extremes. It was an effort to avoid the obvious problems of each of the extreme positions. The various approaches that were ultimately deemed wrong by the majority are discussed later in some detail. It is important to learn the various positions and the way they were viewed by those who held what became the orthodox position.

Ebionites—Jewish Christians

On the fully human end of the spectrum were the Ebionites (EH-bee-oh-nites). There is no clear understanding of the source of the name, and there are no written documents explaining their theology. All that we know of the group comes from the writings of people who considered them heretics. It is clear that they considered themselves Jewish followers of Jesus. They observed the Jewish laws, including requiring all males to be circumcised and to follow the Jewish dietary laws.

We see in Acts 15:5 that some early church leaders believed all Christians must be circumcised and follow the Jewish dietary laws. In spite of his early resistance, James the Just eventually sided with the apostle Paul, and the Jerusalem Council's decision that Gentile converts did not need to be circumcised was transmitted in a letter (Acts 15:27–29). In spite of this, Jewish Christians were still expected to follow all of the Jewish law. This group presumably formed the beginning of the Ebionite sect.

The Ebionites represent the fully human end of the spectrum on the nature of Jesus. They denied that Jesus was born of a virgin or that he existed in some way with God before his birth. For the Ebionites, Jesus was the adopted Son of God. Since Ebionites focused on Jewish law, they believed that what set Jesus apart was that he had followed the law perfectly. Because he was free of sin, his sacrificial death on the cross satisfied God's punishment of death on all sons of Adam. The resurrection of Jesus was a sign that God had accepted his sacrifice. The Ebionites also believed that Jesus's death eliminated the need for the imperfect sacrifice of animals at the temple. Since the temple sacrifice of animals was part of the process of animal slaughter, Ebionites were also vegetarians.

The Ebionites did not accept the apostle Paul or any of his writings. His theology was completely at odds with their beliefs. Ehrman suggests that they had a version of the Gospel of Matthew that did not contain some of the material in the modern version. Ehrman also concludes from writings against the Ebionites by Epiphanius of Cyprus that they had at least one additional Gospel, which included quotations from Jesus against eating meat. The Gospels make it clear that John the Baptist was a vegetarian, and tradition says that Jesus's brother James was one also. So there is adequate support for the idea that Jesus could also have followed this path and that the Ebionites might have been correct in their interpretation of Jesus's actual teachings. However, it is clear that the requirements of following the Jewish law, being circumcised, and becoming a vegetarian would not have been popular. It is not surprising that this brand of Christianity did not sweep through the Roman Empire. But it may well represent the form closest to Jesus's actual practice during his life.

Marcionites—Anti-Jewish Christians

On the other end of the spectrum were the Marcionites (MAR-see-oh-nites). They take their name from a second-century preacher named Marcion. The Marcionites denied the humanity of Jesus. For them, he was God appearing in the illusion of human form. This position is also called Docetism. Jesus was God appearing on earth as a human but still only God. He had no actual human flesh.

The Marcionites also denied any connection between Christianity and Judaism, even to the point that they did not accept the God of the Jews as the God of Jesus. It is not hard to reach the conclusion that the God of the Jews and the Old Testament is somehow different from the God of Jesus and the apostle Paul. The God of the Old Testament takes vengeance for wrongdoing

(Gen. 6:7). He brings a flood that kills virtually all life (Gen. 7:17-24). He rains fire on cities (Gen. 19:24) and repeatedly punishes the Jewish people with exile and destruction for their failures (see, for example, 2 Kings 21:10-15 and 2 Kings 24:1-4). The God of Jesus is a God of love and forgiveness. It is challenging to reconcile these two images, though God does rescue the Israelites from Egypt, and the Psalms show other aspects of God. The Marcionites solved the problem by concluding that there were two different Gods. The Jewish God was a lesser, tribal God who created the physical world and gave the Jews the law. The God of Jesus was the greater God, who only entered the world in Jesus. Since the world was the creation of the Jewish God, the Marcionites concluded that Jesus could not be human at all. He must be the new God and could not be corrupted by being human since that would connect him to the world.

Marcionites did not accept the Jewish scriptures. The apostle Paul's teaching that people are saved by their faith in God was taken to the extreme by the Marcionites. The God of the Jews condemned people to death, but those who had faith in Jesus were saved from death and could have eternal life with the God of Jesus through his resurrection. The apostle Paul was viewed as the only person who truly conveyed the meaning of Jesus's life and death. Paul's conversion on the road to Damascus was viewed by Marcion as a necessary action by Jesus to purge the Church of Jewish components. Since all the original apostles were Jewish, the apostle Paul (who, ironically, was Jewish) was chosen to spread the true word of the God of Jesus.

Marcion and his followers accepted only 11 books as forming the sacred canon of scripture. This consisted of ten of the letters attributed to the apostle Paul found in our New Testament (excluding 1 and 2 Timothy and Titus), and an edited version of the Gospel of Luke that had many portions removed that did not agree with Marcion's beliefs. There were even problems with the letters of the apostle Paul, which sometimes quote the Old

Testament. Marcion's answer to this was to assume that these passages were inserted by scribes who copied the documents (Ehrman 2003, p. 109).

Marcionites were present in the Roman Empire even in the fifth century, so it is highly probable that Marcion's views would have been well known at the Council of Nicaea, even though the proto-orthodox community considered them heretical. The appeal of Marcionite Christianity in the Roman Empire was also limited, but for a different reason than the Ebionite version. Ehrman argues that the Romans revered religions that were ancient and that they were suspicious of new sects and religious groups (Ehrman 2003, p. 112). Since Marcionites were completely separate from Judaism, they were clearly a new religion. Thus, their appeal was limited. The Marcionites would counter that the scriptures used by the other Christians were fabricated to graft the true faith in Jesus onto Jewish roots to make it more appealing in the Roman Empire.

Clearly, the only form of Christianity that would grow in the empire had to be somewhere between these extremes. It was necessary to retain the Jewish roots of Jesus and the Old Testament. At the same time, it was important to embrace the theology of the apostle Paul, which made the faith more accessible by avoiding the Jewish laws. The meeting between the apostle Paul and the apostles in Jerusalem (Gal. 2 and Acts 15), at which Paul received permission to preach to the Gentiles without the need for them to adopt the Jewish laws, was the first attempt to reconcile these two goals. But the debate continued for centuries.

Gnostics

Another important group of early Christians was the Gnostics, who also differentiated between the God of the Old Testament and the God of Jesus. Their cosmology was often complex. They had a very dualistic theology, with a pantheon of good and bad gods. They also saw Jesus as a dual being, part human and part God. Their solution to the problem of how God could die on the cross was to deny that it happened. For many Gnostics, the divine part of Jesus left his physical body before his death on the cross so that only the human part died. The divine part of Jesus could therefore be the one Good God and yet Jesus could also be human. A fuller discussion of Gnosticism is provided in appendix 1 of this book. The Gnostics' complex view of God as an eternal, unknowable, and undefinable spirit who spawned a large number of lesser spiritual beings probably has its roots in Greek Platonism of the first and second centuries, which had a similar cosmology for the creation of the world. Within this context, it was easier to consider Jesus a lesser spirit when compared with his Father, the Greater God. This direction leads to polytheism, which was another heresy that the Christians could not tolerate.

Proto-orthodox writers of the third and fourth centuries C.E. spent more time railing against the Gnostics and Valentineans than against any other sects. This implies that they were considered a serious threat to the proto-orthodox position. By that point, the Ebionites, Christians who saw Christianity as a part of Judaism, had been marginalized, although there were many such documents still in circulation in the 50 years leading up to the Council of Nicaea. Thus, anything speculative about Jesus that still exists can be assumed to be something that would have been available at the time.

The marriage of the extremes required a compromise on how to view Jesus's relationship to God. Jesus could not be only man or only God. But the spectrum of choices was still broad. Arius and the Adoptionists took the humanity of Jesus as their starting point and then endowed him with divine nature when God adopted him. The timing of this varied. Some believed it happened when he was baptized by John the Baptist and a dove descended on him from heaven. Others placed the adoption at his birth. Others used the wording of the Gospel of John to argue that the divine aspect of Jesus had existed as a part of God from the Creation and that the human Jesus was not really adopted but that the Word became flesh in Jesus. The criticism of this position lay in the fact that it made Jesus of lesser status than the eternal creator God. This is called subordinationism because it suggests that Jesus was in a lesser position than God the Father. Of course, the son is traditionally subordinate to the father, so there is an undeniable logic to this position. But it could lead to polytheism.

The modern concept of the Trinity is the ultimate solution arrived at by the Christian church. This concept walks the knife edge between the opposing points of view and tries to avoid the heresy that lies so close on either side.

Areas of Agreement and Disagreement

In the early fourth century, there were some things about which virtually all Christians could agree:[4]

1. There was only one true God, though many people worship false gods.
2. Jesus was clearly human but somehow more than human. He had a special relationship with God.
3. Somehow, Jesus had brought salvation to humanity, though there was no agreement on how to express this conviction in precise theological language.
4. The scriptures were the authoritative source of authority for Christians, though there is evidence that people of faith sometimes "corrected" writings that didn't always make sense from their perspective.

The disagreements began when Christian theologians began to try to define the relationship between Jesus and God more precisely. The Church probably had little time to engage in speculation and introspection on the details while under constant threat of death from the Roman Empire. After this threat was lifted, Christians discovered they needed a theology that could be used to articulate and explain their creeds and beliefs.

Those who worked out this theology were known as apologists (not in the sense of apologizing for but in the sense of making a case for their

beliefs). The language that evolved in this environment can be confusing today and must have also been so then, at least to some Christians. The fundamental problem was the conflict between monotheistic belief in one God with a unique nature different from and transcendent of human beings and the understanding that Jesus, a human being, was in some sense divine as well.

The struggle at Nicaea is to find a way to suggest that Jesus was both divine and human, given that humanity and divinity were never to be identified with or made equal to each other. Humanity was always *created*, God was always *creator*, and an ontological gap always existed between them. Therefore, if Jesus was human (as the Church insisted he was), then he had to be created. There was a time when he was not, as Arius insisted. But if he was created, he could not be divine. And, if he was not divine, he did not have the power to save humanity. However, if he wasn't human, then he had no intrinsic relationship with the very humanity he came to save, and he would not have been needed to acquire salvation for humanity, since God could have done that without the aid of a human being.

Two Greek words that came into play in the discussion were *ousious* (OO-see-us), or sometimes *ousia*, and *hypostasis* (hi-po-STAY-sis). On one level, these words seem to mean almost the same thing, the essence or substance of something. These words were used in the attempt to define how Jesus should be viewed, and the results were often conflicting just in their language. Was God a single *ousious* with multiple *hypostases* or a single *hypostasis* with multiple *ousioi*? Both terms appear to have been used and appear to be a distinction without a difference.

The deeper question was how God's *ousia* could be shared with other beings without detracting from God's oneness and transcendence. How could Jesus be both human and divine at the same time without subverting God's divinity or Jesus's humanity? This controversy was at the center of the debate at Nicaea.

On one side of the debate were Eusebius of Nicomedia, Eusebius of Caesarea, Arius, and others who believed that God and Jesus represented two different *hypostases*. God was the first of these, and the Son, Christ, the Word, was a second *hypostasis* that was in some way derived from or created by God. The details of the origin of the Son were not clear, but it was clear that God was not divided to form the Son, nor was the Son equal to the fullness of God's divinity. Jesus came after God, or as the Arians would say, "there was a time when he was not." In this construction, the Son was the *hypostasis* that interacted with humanity throughout the scriptures. It was the Son/Word who spoke to Abraham, wrestled with Jacob, and spoke to the prophets. The Son/Word became visible when it entered into Jesus.[5] The Son was clearly in some way subordinate to the Father, and this idea is supported by many passages of scripture (see John 14:28, for example). For the Alexandrian faction, the idea that Jesus was subordinate to God and not his equal was also problematic and was known as subordinationism.

The salvation brought by Jesus in this system was less related to his death on the cross and more to his moral life and willingness to suffer for humanity. His life was an example for humans to follow, and through the knowledge of God brought by the Son and by following his example, Christians were saved. The Gnostics might have argued that the knowledge that Jesus brought was in itself the core of our salvation. The Holy Spirit was pretty much an afterthought in this system.

The problem of the dual-*hypostasis* approach is that it flies in the face of the fundamental monotheism of Christianity. It is difficult to find language that supposes God and the Son are two different essences but still asserts that God is One.

The alternate system accepted only one *hypostasis* for God. This avoids the danger of slipping into polytheism, but it complicates the issue of the Son and his connection to the *hypostasis* of God. Athanasius was a major proponent of this theology and articulated the role of the Son when he said,

"God became man so man could become divine."[6] The purpose of God entering into Jesus in the form of his Word was to reunite God with all humanity. This allows the passages in which Jesus speaks of being less than God or that Jesus is not privy to God's secrets (see Mark 13:32, for example) to be interpreted in terms of divine humanity being less than God. God has acted through his Word becoming flesh in Jesus to elevate humanity, returning humans to their original state before they were separated from God after the Fall in the Garden of Eden.

The Son/Word shares in the *hypostasis* of God, and salvation could be viewed as the Word or *hypostasis* of God entering all Christians. But this way of putting it runs into the other heresy of identifying God with humanity, making them one with each other. This is heresy because it denies the transcendence of God over all created things, which would include humanity. As close as human beings and God come to each other, they never become ontologically one, a position that would deny the difference between Creator and creature.

At the heart of the debate is whether *any* terms drawn from the Greek language are adequate to express what, in the philosophical terms of the day, was a contradiction: the divine becomes human and/or the human becomes divine without subtracting from God's oneness and full divinity. Perhaps you simply say that the confusing language of the time was insufficient to express multiple Christian convictions or beliefs in a philosophically coherent way.

Salvation

The two competing interpretations of the *hypostasis* of God and the Son have additional implications. The dual-*hypostasis* system requires action on the part of believers to live a moral life following the example of Jesus. God through Jesus has shown the way, which each Christian must follow to achieve salvation. In the single-*hypostasis* system, God, rather than the individual Christians, is active. God has joined himself to humanity, and his action elevates Christians to divinity by simply accepting the gift of God. There are ample passages of scripture that support both interpretations. The letters of the apostle Paul support God as the active agent, whereas the more Jewish-centered Christian tradition, such as the letters attributed to James the Just, focus on the need for Christians to follow the example of Jesus. Even after the Church arrived at a consensus on the mystery of Jesus and God, the debate on the nature of salvation continued. In fact, the debate is still active in the Church today.

Creeds—Dealing with Heresy

Constantine decided to call for the council of bishops in Nicaea in order to solve several major heresies that were dividing the Church. One, the Novatianist controversy, has been discussed already. The other was the Arian controversy that grew out of the conflict between Arius and Bishop Alexander of Egypt. Some years ago, both Arius and Alexander had been candidates for the position of bishop in Alexandria. Alexander won that contest, but Arius was very popular with the people and continued to work as a priest. Alexander may have been jealous of the popularity of Arius, but at the core of the conflict were their views on the nature of Jesus, the Son of God.

Arius and Alexander had different views on the relationship between God and Jesus, and Alexander eventually tried to excommunicate Arius and forced him to leave Egypt. Arius made his way to Palestine and took up residence with Eusebius of Caesarea. Alexander continued his efforts to remove Arius from the Church, and a council of bishops was convened in Antioch to examine Arius and his supporters. The bishops at Antioch voted to excommunicate Arius and all who believed as he did that Jesus was not coeternal with God. The Letter of the Council of Antioch is available for you to read. (See the link to the original document in part 5 of this book.)

The excommunicated bishops were powerful people, including Eusebius of Caesarea and Eusebius of Nicomedia. They refused to accept the decision of the Antioch Council. They argued before Constantine that the bishops attending the Antioch Council were not representative of the whole Church and that their decision was not binding on them. Constantine responded by convening a much larger council in Nicaea in an attempt to put all of the contentious issues to rest for the last time.

So what do the bishops at Nicaea believe? There is certainly a range of opinion, but the majority of opinions are not too far from the mainstream of modern Christianity. Both the Apostles' Creed and the creed written by Irenaeus see God as having three manifestations: Father, Son, and Holy Spirit. Both creeds have separate statements for each of them. The bishops at Nicaea will be guided by these documents as they formulate a new creed for the Church.

The council faces a choice on whether to write a general creed that will cast a wide net to include a diversity of Christians or to sharpen the language to exclude all who don't subscribe to the majority view. Alexander and his supporters, as well as those who wish to remove the Novatianists from the Church, would like to use the creed as a way to eliminate these ideas from the Church altogether. The Arians and Novatianists share the desire to purify the Church but differ in the core beliefs that would be required by the creed. Constantine's desire for unity clearly conflicted with the desire of all groups who sought to eliminate their opponents by using the new creed.

There are only a few issues to resolve in reaching a consensus that would include the majority of fourth-century Christians. Jesus was God Incarnate (incarnate means "in the flesh or bodily," literally *in meat*). In some way, God had entered the world through the Word, Jesus, and had thereby become flesh. The points of contention are:

- What is the true nature of Jesus? Was he God, man, or both at once?
- If Jesus had a human nature, then when did Jesus become Christ (i.e., the anointed one, or

the divine being)? There are lots of choices, all with ardent supporters:

- at his conception
- at his birth
- at his baptism
- at his resurrection from the dead and ascension into heaven
- from the creation of the universe
- before the creation of the universe but not forever along with God
- from all eternity along with God himself.

The divine nature of Jesus, the Word, or Logos is the way that God entered into Jesus. The major contention is actually when the Word began to be a part of God. Alexander argued that the Word was always present within God. Arius believed that the Word was created by God before he began the creation of the universe. This may seem like a small point, but it was enough to threaten the unity of the Church. The issue of when the Word entered into Jesus was seen as less important than the ultimate relationship between the Word and God.

THE BIBLE AND OTHER EARLY CHRISTIAN WRITINGS

The word "Bible" derives from the word for papyrus (*biblios*). At the time of the Council of Nicaea, there was no Bible as we have it today. The issue of which writings of the Church were authoritative and useful was far from settled. Most Christians used a Greek version of the Old Testament called the LXX or Septuagint, which included the Hebrew scriptures of the Tanakh plus additional books, including Judith, Tobit, and the books of the Maccabees.

The decision on which texts to include in the canon was not made until well after the Council of Nicaea, though by the time of the council, a general consensus was beginning to emerge. If any of the diverse groups discussed here had come to dominate the Church, the nature of the Bible could have been very different. Texts were selected for inclusion only if they supported the developing orthodoxy of the latter fourth century C.E. and later.

Fourth-century biblical scholars such as Eusebius were still actively studying the Septuagint and comparing it with existing Hebrew texts and other translations to ensure that it was a true representation of the Word of God. They often speak of "correcting" the texts being considered for inclusion in what later became the canon of official writings comprising the Bible based on their own theological and linguistic knowledge. Thus, the product of their work is filtered through their theology. Their noncanonical writings often quote extensively from the Septuagint to support both the antiquity of Christianity and the Messianic role of Jesus.

The New Testament canon was not established until the end of the fourth century, by a council held at Rome in 382 C.E. Fifty years earlier, at the time of the Council of Nicaea, there were many writings, of varying quality and authority, circulating in the churches. In his book *Lost Christianities*, Ehrman has compiled a fairly comprehensive list of the documents (Ehrman 2003, pp. xi–xv). These would have been available to some or all of the Church in the fourth century C.E. Tables 1 to 3 list the known texts identified by Ehrman. Most of the authorship notes in these tables are from Ehrman, with the exception of those on the letters of the apostle Paul.

Tables 1–3 include various other Gospels that detailed the life and teaching of Jesus but were not included in the New Testament. There are also a number of books of Acts that described the acts of various apostles after Jesus's resurrection, and a range of letters written by or attributed to the apostles and others. By the time of the Council of Nicaea, there was a growing consensus among the bishops that was very close to the current twenty-seven books of the New Testament. However, orthodoxy was by no means universal, as can be inferred from the constant attacks on those who did not agree on the existing writings.

Although the basic outline of the modern New Testament was well established for most in the mainstream of Christianity, many factions still

TABLE 1 Available Gospels and their probable dates from Ehrman (2003). Canonical documents are boldfaced.

Gospel of	Approximate date (c.e.) (Ehrman 2003)	Comments based on Ehrman (2003, pp. xi–xii) and other sources where there is disagreement
Mark	**70–80**	**Earliest Gospel**
Secret Gospel of Mark	58?	Supposed secret information on Jesus and rituals of membership with homoerotic overtones
Matthew	**80–90**	
Luke	**80–90**	
John	**90–100**	
Nazarenes	Early second century	Aramaic Matthew without first two chapters. Used by Ebionite Christians
Peter	Early second century	Fragment only
Thomas (Coptic)	Early second century	114 sayings of Jesus, some probably authentic and some possible Gnostic additions
Infancy Gospel of Thomas	Early second century	Probably historical fiction about Jesus's childhood
Papyrus Egerton 2	Early second century	Fragment
Hebrews	Early second century	Life narrative of Jesus, including Gnostic and Jewish ideas used in Egypt
Ebionites	Early second century	Includes antisacrifice ideas of the Ebionites
Egyptians	Early second century	Used by non-Jewish Christians stressing ascetic ideals
James	Mid-second century	Birth narrative of Jesus
Truth	Mid-second century	Gnostic Gospel
Epistle of the Apostles	Mid-second century	Anti-Gnostic emphasizing the idea that Jesus was a flesh and blood human before and after resurrection
Mary	Second century	Mary Magdalene reveals her vision granting her permission to convey Jesus's secret teachings
Gospel of the Savior	Late second century	Coptic
Philip	Third century	Gnostic mystical reflections

TABLE 2 Texts in the "Acts" genre and their dates of composition. Canonical documents are boldfaced.

Act	Approximate date (C.E.) (Ehrman 2003)	Comments
Acts of the Apostles	**80–90**	**Account of early ministry of the apostles and Paul's mission to the Gentiles**
Acts of Pilate	Mid-second century	Account of Jesus's trial that exonerates Pilate
Acts of John	End second century	Apostle John's missionary activities
Acts of Peter	End second century	Apostle Peter's missionary activities and his fight against Simon Magus
Acts of Thecla	End second century	Deeds, persecution, and miraculous escape of Paul's most famous female convert
Acts of Paul	End second century	Includes miracles of Paul, the Acts of Thecla, and 3 Corinthians
Acts of Thomas	Third century	Missionary journey of Jesus's brother Thomas in India

cherished books that were not included. Since all documents were copied by hand, there were also different versions of books. Thus, biblical scholars could "correct" documents based on their theology and change earlier ideas that did not fit their beliefs in the name of correcting errors in transmission or translation. Some of those capable of copying the texts were well-educated Christians who were schooled in Greek philosophy, and this may have led them to attempt to reconcile some of the philosophical inconsistencies in the early Christian writings. Some others were only semiliterate and made unintentional copying errors. Ehrman (*Misquoting Jesus* and *Lost Christianities*) points out numerous examples of additions and deletions to the Gospels and letters along with some details on how bad the copying process could be. At least 100,000 variations between the early texts have been identified. The vast majority of these are insignificant errors in spelling, dropping a line, abbreviating a word, and so forth. Because so many copies of ancient manuscripts have been discovered, we have reasonable confidence that most of the New Testament is true to the original authors.

There are numerous other letters that were not included in the New Testament. Some were such obvious forgeries that, even in the third century, they could be identified and discredited. But some books now considered forgeries were widely accepted.

The challenge for students in the game is similar to that of scholars both today and in the fourth century. When there are multiple copies of a document that disagree on some fundamental point, how does one determine which is the authoritative one? The first answer is to look for consistency of ideas. If the apostle Paul in one place says that women who talk in church must cover their heads and then later in the same document says that women should never talk in church, one must conclude that the statements are inconsistent. Both cannot be correct. Students in this game may present various wordings of the scriptures that existed before 325 C.E. to the council to defend their positions and claim the copies they have are the authoritative ones. Rather than an argument about interpretation of an agreed on set of words, the argument will then become one on

TABLE 3 Letters and other writings and their dates of composition. Canonical documents are boldfaced.

Text	Author/Date (c.e.)	Description
Romans **1 & 2 Corinthians** **Galatians Philippians** **1 Thessalonians Philemon**	**Apostle Paul 50–57**	**Considered genuine letters of Paul**
Ephesians **2 Thessalonians Colossians**		**Authorship contested**
1 Timothy **2 Timothy** **Titus**	**Late first century and early second century**	**Written in Paul's name by later authors. Some contain ideas in direct conflict with Paul's genuine letters.**
Secret Book of John	Late second century	Gnostic book detailing their cosmology
Revelation of John	**Late first century**	**Apocalyptic vision of the second coming of Christ and the Judgment of God**
Treatise on the Resurrection	Late second century	Gnostic explanation of death and spiritual resurrection
Didache	First century	Manual of Christian practice
1 Clement	96	Letter from bishop of Rome to Corinthians
2 Clement	Mid-second century	Proto-orthodox interpretation of Isaiah
3 Corinthians	Late second century	Attack on Gnostics
Epistle of Barnabas	130–140	Proto-orthodox, argues that Judaism is a false religion
Letter of Ptolemy to Flora	Late second century	Letter from Gnostic explaining Gnostic understanding of Old Testament
1, 2, and 3 John	Late first century	Possibly written by same author as Gospel of John. No author is identified by name in the texts.
1 Peter	First century	Attributed to Peter, warning against false teaching and encouraging Christians under persecution
2 Peter	Second century	Later work attributed to Peter
Jude	First century	Attributed to Jude, the brother of James and Jesus
Hebrews	First century	Argument for the superiority of Christianity over Judaism. Authorship unknown but attributed to Paul in the fourth century. Also attributed to Priscilla by some.
James	First century	Attributed to James the Just, but scholars doubt this based on style and content

Virtually the entire existing body of early Christian writings is available at the web site http://www.earlychristianwritings .com/.

which wording is consistent with all that is known about Jesus. A few examples from *Misquoting Jesus* will suffice to show how these changes can influence the discussions at Nicaea.

An example of a significant addition is the story in John 7:53–8:12 of Jesus's conversation with the woman caught in adultery, which is not present in the earliest versions of the text (Ehrman 2005, p. 63). A later version contains the story as a marginal note. Possibly someone reading the text thought of it as an example of what he felt the message of Jesus was in that passage. Later copyists moved the marginal note into the actual text, where it became part of the actual Gospel, but the scribes placed the story in three different places in various manuscripts of the Gospels: after John 7:52, after John 21:25, and even in Luke 21:38 (Ehrman 2005, p. 65).

Some of the editorial changes were made to make specific theological points. Ehrman notes a number of these in *Misquoting Jesus*. A few examples will suffice to make the point, and the reader is referred to Ehrman (2005, pp. 151–75) for more details.

1 Timothy 3:16, "God made manifest in flesh" (King James Version),[7] appears in later versions such as the Revised Standard Version (RSV)[8] as "(Christ) who was manifested in the flesh." The difference in Greek between "God" and "who" is the change from ΘΣ to ΟΣ. This is clearly an easy error to make in copying but makes a large difference in meaning (Ehrman 2005, p. 157).

Mark 1:11 and Luke 3:23 both have the phrase "You are my beloved Son, in whom I am well pleased" immediately after Jesus's baptism. However, the quotations of this text that appear in commentaries from the second and third centuries all say, "You are my beloved Son, today have I begotten thee." The earlier form clearly fits with the Adoptionist view of Jesus becoming God's Son at his baptism and would have been revised later by anti-Arian scribes (Ehrman 2005, p. 159).

There are several places where the text was changed from "his parents" to "Joseph and his mother." This occurs in Luke 2:33, when Jesus is presented at the temple, and later, in Luke 2:43, where "his parents" did not know he had stayed behind in the temple at age 12 (Ehrman 2005, p. 158). This could be significant to the debate at Nicaea. If Jesus was a human adopted by God, then Joseph could be his parent. The change to "Joseph and his mother" specifically denies that Joseph was Jesus's father.

A second line of argument to support a particular wording of a text is to have the same position represented by the writings of several independent authors. In the discussion of whether God and Jesus have the same substance, the challenge is to find language supporting this position in several independent places. A single statement in one source is probably not enough to be convincing, since it could have been added to support the position. The same arguments will need to be made by students who want to introduce as authoritative books that are not in the New Testament. The test of consistency and confirmation by multiple authors will be useful for students who are trying to make up their minds. In the Latin Vulgate Bible with Translation, 1 John 5:7 says:

There are three that bear witness in heaven, the Father, the Word, and the Holy Ghost, and these three are one.

This statement does not appear in early copies of the text and is thought to be a later addition to support the emerging doctrine of the Trinity.

Another example is from Luke 5:37–39, where Jesus tells the parable of the old wineskins. The RSV Bible has this statement:

And no one puts new wine into old wineskins; otherwise the new wine will burst the skins and will be spilled, and the skins will be destroyed. But new wine must be put into fresh wineskins. And no one after drinking old wine desires new wine, but says, "The old is good."

This parable is interpreted to mean that Jesus is saying that the salvation he brings is better than that of the Jewish law. But the scribes were confused by the "old is good" statement. That would imply that Judaism was better than Christianity, so the last sentence, verse 39, was deleted in these manuscripts (Ehrman 2005, p. 96).

A final example is relevant to the Arian heresy. Matthew 24:36 in the King James Version says:

But of that day and hour knoweth no man, no, not the angels of heaven, but my Father only.
The Revised Standard Version has this as:
But about that day and hour no one knows, neither the angels of heaven, nor the Son, but only the Father.

This sentence relates to when the end of the age will come. If God the Father and Jesus are one being, how can it be that the Father knows the day of the end of the world and the Son does not? The scribes solved this problem by deleting the three words "nor the Son" (Ehrman 2005, p. 95). This eliminates the obvious question raised by the original text. Most modern translations of the Bible, like the Revised Standard Version, have footnotes noting these changes, and in most cases, the scholars who prepare the translations have tried to determine the oldest and most authoritative text for their work. However, the KJV relied on the edited text.

The original Greek texts had no spaces, punctuation, or capital letters. Ehrman uses the example *godisnowhere*, which could be read as *god is now here* or *god is nowhere*. The fact that some scribes could not actually read the texts and just copied letter by letter made proofreading difficult. And the changes were so pronounced that both Christian writers such as Origen and their critics

such as Celsus noted the fact. Ehrman (2005, p. 52) gives some examples:

Some believers, as though from a drinking bout, go so far as to oppose themselves and alter the original text of the gospel three or four or several times over, and they change its character to enable them to deny difficulties in the face of criticism. (*Against Celsus* 2.27)

So my opinion is that the Gospels in being copied over and over again by persons who did not know the language became confused at this point in the quotation of the Psalm mentioned above. (*Origen Commentary on Matthew* xvi, 19 X, 542, I-6, Kolstermann, as quoted in Metzger 1968, p.100)

Some of the roles in this game include specific information on alternate versions of scripture to buttress specific points that the students will make. This may challenge you in the game sessions, since instead of arguing various interpretations of the same text, you may well be arguing various wordings of the same text. You should be prepared to support a specific wording on the basis of its consistency with other passages. A single passage alone will probably not prove convincing. The supplemental material in *Misquoting Jesus* and *Lost Christianities*, which is the source of these references in the roles, can help you address the underlying reasons for these changes.

It is possible for you to rewrite any short scripture in a way that makes it convey the meaning you perceive. The words you read in the English translation of the scriptures are the result of a translation process that includes interpretation based on the meaning perceived by the translator. Since most students lack both the knowledge of ancient Greek and access to original texts, you can reinterpret a passage to be consistent with your understanding of the intended meaning. As in the case of the variations known in the literature, it is vital that you look for consistency between the proposed language and the rest of the document in question.

Reading assignments for the game will include several ancient documents that have only recently come to light. Around 390 C.E., after the Council of Nicaea, Emperor Theodosius made Nicaean Christianity the only religion allowed in the empire. At this point, both traditional Roman religions and other forms of Christianity were officially banned. Books that supported ideas inconsistent with the Nicaean interpretation were systematically destroyed or abandoned. People who held such texts could be summarily executed for having them. A large collection of books hidden in Egypt during this period was discovered at Nag Hammadi in 1945, and these books have greatly added to our understanding of the diversity of Christian opinion at the time. Many of these texts are classified as Gnostic, and the most important of them is the Gospel of Thomas. The collection also contains the Gospel of Mary Magdalene, in which she claims to have been Jesus's favorite disciple. Students with Gnostic roles should pay special attention to these documents. It is thought that these texts were buried to prevent their destruction during the purge of heretical texts following the edict of Theodosius.

Because there was such a wide diversity of texts of the same book in circulation, some students in the Nicaea game may have arrived at the council with texts that support their theological position and that refute the positions of their opponents. This would not be unexpected. When conflicting texts appear in the course of the argument, the council members will have to decide for themselves which text is more authoritative. The most respected biblical scholar in Nicaea is Eusebius of Caesarea. He has access to one of the finest libraries of scripture in the world. The other person with a sharp intellect and access to a rich library is Athanasius. He has access to the library at Alexandria and is just starting what will be an exemplary career as a writer. As a result of the uncertainty about what the texts actually say, the debate at

Nicaea may address not only what the words say but which words are the right words. The council will have to decide these issues based on their understanding and faith and the weight of evidence for consistency.

As noted in tables 1–3, many of the texts we now have were written in the second or even the third century but were attributed to Jesus's apostles or other Christian heroes. Ideas of authorship were very different, and the attribution may indicate that they were drawn from oral traditions tracing to the author or reflect a school of thought traced to the designated author. The attribution to an apostle would also lend them credibility since the primary defense against heresy was the Apostolic tradition. The Gospel of Thomas is a classic example. Writing texts was a major way that the various Christian communities promulgated and argued for their theological positions. Again, this is not a foreign idea. One need only visit the nonfiction section of any bookstore to see the way authors try to convince the public of their interpretations of events. American presidential candidates can hardly begin their quest for office without writing a book in which they put their personal spin on the events of their lives and current events. These early Christian writings are hardly different. Newly uncovered documents, like the Gospel of Judas, continue to emerge from archaeological research. Recently developed techniques to read documents written on parchment, which were later erased and reused, have also added to the collection of early writings. Recovery of these documents is important because some early documents are known only because they were quoted in documents that attacked them.

What is clear from the survey of surviving documents is that a diverse literature of Christian thought had evolved before the Council of Nicaea. Once an orthodox position emerged with the power of the Roman Empire behind it, anything that conflicted with the orthodox position was disposed of. The burning of books supporting nonorthodox theology was a way to eliminate the conflicting points of view and enforce orthodoxy throughout the Church. Rewriting and editing was a less dramatic but more pervasive method.

THE RISE OF CONSTANTINE[9]

War and Politics

In the year 293 C.E., the government of the Roman Empire was reformed to improve governance of the sprawling region. (See map of the Roman Empire in part 1.) The empire was divided into two parts, each with its own administration. There would be two emperors (Augusti), assisted by Caesars. This group was referred to as the Imperial College (IC). The leadership was referred to as the tetrarchy. In theory, when an Augustus retired, his assistant Caesar would be promoted and a new Caesar selected. This happened in 303, when Diocletian and Maximian retired from their positions as Augusti and Constantius and Galerius were promoted to Augustus. This would allow the appointment of two new Caesars and institute a regular process of succession.

Unfortunately, there was a controversy over who would become Caesar, with three candidates for the two posts. Also, Maximian didn't really want to retire. The resulting controversy was settled by a series of civil wars that didn't end until Constantine had eliminated all competition and ended the tetrarchy in favor of a single Augustus over the whole Roman Empire.

Flavius Constantius, the father of Constantine, served in Syria and became governor of Dalmatia (modern Croatia) and later prefect of Gaul (modern France). Constantine was born around 272 or 273 C.E., the illegitimate son of Constantius. Constantine's mother, Helena, was the teenage daughter of an innkeeper who was given to Constantius by the innkeeper as a favor while he was an officer in the Roman army staying at the inn. Constantine was reunited with his father as a teenager and given an education in his father's household.

In 293, Constantius was appointed Caesar in the Imperial College under Emperor Maximian.

Constantine was 20 years old when his father was named Caesar, and Constantine would have been presumed to succeed his father as Caesar and eventually Augustus. Constantine distinguished himself as an effective soldier and popular leader in the East under Diocletian and Galerius.

Constantius appears to have been favorably disposed toward the Christians and had failed to pursue orders issued by the Augustus to persecute them. As soon as he was promoted to Augustus, he had Constantine sent to join him in France. Constantine distinguished himself in a bold campaign to defeat the Picts in Scotland. By the end of that campaign in 306, Constantius was ill, and he soon died. At his death, the soldiers proclaimed Constantine Augustus. This was the beginning of a civil war that would last for 12 years as various military leaders attempted to eliminate their rivals.

The year 310 opened with six men claiming the position of Augustus: Galerius, Maximinus, and Licinius in the East and Constantine, Maximian, and Maxentius in the West. Maximian tried and failed to depose Constantine and committed suicide. Then Maxentius declared war on Constantine while Licinius was distracted fighting in the East. Constantine began a campaign against Maxentius in Italy and shrewdly did not follow the usual scorched earth policy of such campaigns. Thus, he made friends in Italy. In October, Maxentius was defeated and drowned in the Tiber.

In 311, when Galerius died (see Eusebius, *History of the Church*, book IX, chapter 10, sections 14–15 for a colorful account of his illness, which was possibly colon cancer), Maximinus immediately began to take over the territory of Galerius.

Constantine then solidified an alliance with Licinius by having him marry his half-sister, Constantia. Licinius attacked Maximinus and defeated him. Maximinus committed suicide in July, leaving only two members of the IC. Licinius followed up his victory with a major purge in which all descendants of Galerius, Diocletian, and Maximinus who might claim positions in the IC were killed. The purge also seems to have removed many others who were active in the Great Persecution of Christians initiated by Diocletian. At this point, there were only two Augusti, Constantine in the West and Licinius in the East.

In 315 and 316, the two began to plot against each other for supremacy. This developed into open warfare in 316. Neither Licinius nor Constantine was able to win a decisive victory against the other during a series of battles over the next five years. In 324, Constantine finally defeated Licinius, and he surrendered in Nicomedia. Constantine allowed him to retire in Thessalonica in northern Greece (probably as a favor to his half-sister, who was married to Licinius). In spite of Constantine's promise to spare Licinius, he later had him killed along with his young son, who was a potential rival for power. At this point, Constantine was the undisputed single ruler of the entire empire.

Constantine and the Christians

When Constantine succeeded Constantius in 306, he immediately stopped the persecution of Christians in the area he controlled (Britain, Gaul, and Spain). He allowed them freedom of worship and restored all property that had been taken from them during the Great Persecution of Diocletian. He also enlisted the Christian population of Italy with promises of religious freedom during his campaign against Maxentius.

In the first decade of Constantine's rule (306–316 C.E.), his edicts and letters only speak of his belief in a Supreme Being. It can be argued that he was a superstitious person and felt from observation that the God of the Christians was both powerful and responsible for his own rise to power. Only around 324 does Constantine begin to refer to Christ in his letters. Whether this represents a deepening of his understanding of his religious beliefs or simply his sense of freedom to articulate them after Licinius was defeated is not clear.

Constantine had publicly espoused his faith in Christ as the Supreme Being by the time of the Council of Nicaea, but he did not allow himself to be baptized until just before his death. This has led many to take his commitment to the faith with some skepticism. Others argue that late baptism was a common practice (Jones 1964). It is also clear that Constantine refused to practice the traditional Roman religious practices. When he made his triumphal entry into Rome, he did not make the traditional offering at the temple of Jupiter. He also supported the Christian church with great vigor throughout his reign. The Christians of his day tended to romanticize his role and see in his success in uniting the empire the working of the Holy Spirit to bring about the Kingdom of God. His long reign as emperor was also seen as a sign of God's favor.

Constantine was clearly ambitious and ruthless in his rise to power. He had his wife, Fausta, killed and his son, Crispus, executed on questionable charges. He ruthlessly eliminated those who challenged him for power. One of the attractions of the Christian faith may have been its moral code and its tendency toward asceticism. This would be a good way to keep his subjects in line and behaving well. So Christianity was, at least in part, a very utilitarian choice for him no matter how sincere his religious convictions were. According to the Christian tradition, all of his sins would be washed away with baptism. Thus, delaying baptism was a good decision for Constantine.

Constantine's decision to choose Christianity as his preferred religion is a critical point in the development of the Christian church. Historians are divided on his motivation for this action. Centuries of intermittent persecution had done nothing to slow the growth of the Jesus movement. Some areas may have been majority Christian by this time. Churches operated publicly and had begun to amass substantial resources, in part because of the dedication of a membership willing to face martyrdom for their faith. By enlisting the support of the Christians against his political foes, Constantine gained a large and important block of followers.

Various legends (see Eusebius, *Life of Constantine*, book XXVIII) have been recorded about

Constantine's visions of the cross and the words "In this sign conquer" during his conquest of Rome. Whether this is a fact or just a romantic story concocted by Constantine or his apologists is not clear. It is likely that it is something fabricated by Eusebius, who became his leading apologist. (It probably has the same lack of historical credibility as George Washington's chopping down of the cherry tree.)

Constantine was very disturbed when, after supporting the Church with financial resources and making clerics exempt from public service, he discovered that Christians did not agree on fundamental points of their religion. There were strong divisions between bishops from the western parts of the empire (where Constantine had begun his rise to power) and those in the east. Possibly some of the dispute among Christians was caused by the influence of Greek philosophers, particularly Plato, in the eastern parts. Also, the eastern parts had more trade with regions outside the empire, including Persia, with its Zoroastrian religion, and India, which sent Hindu and Buddhist traders. It is possible that Buddhist missionaries were active in some eastern parts of the empire (Klostermaier 1994, p. 18). The cult of Mithras was also popular in the east and in Britain. It was also common in the Roman army. Africa and the east seem to have had a plethora of groups who thought they had the one true Christian religion.

Constantine had called several small councils of bishops to try to settle local issues before calling the Council of Nicaea. By calling the Ecumenical Council of Bishops to meet in Nicaea, he hoped to settle these issues once and for all. After the council reached a conclusion, Constantine had very little patience for divergent views.

INTELLECTUAL POSITIONS REPRESENTED IN THE GAME

The factions that may have played a role at Nicaea are identified by the names of individuals who are most closely associated with these theological positions. However, Arius and Meletius are the only ones who were actually present at Nicaea. The other names here represent people long dead but whose ideas were still held by their followers. The Arian theology is the major point of contention at the council. The Council of Antioch[10] (early 325 C.E.) had ruled that Arius and those who followed his ideas were to be excommunicated. However, the ruling at Antioch was under appeal and had to be confirmed at Nicaea. Arius and his supporters will work to reverse the ruling at Antioch. The major nonorthodox factions who opposed what is now the Trinitarian theology of the Christian church are described briefly in the sections that follow.

Arius and His Supporters

Arius and his followers believe that in his ontological nature or substance, Jesus was fundamentally different from God. The most common point of agreement among this group would be the statement, "There was a time when he (Jesus) was not." Whatever the nature of Jesus, the Christ, he was not "coeternal" with God the Father. God is eternal, undivided, and unknowable. Jesus was his Begotten Son, the Word through whom the universe was created. But the Son is different in some fundamental way from the Father. If Jesus is begotten of the Father, how can he not be different in some essential way? Is a son identical to his father? For Arians, he clearly is not. This group believes that Jesus was the Son of God from before the creation but did not coexist with God forever. For them, God existed before the Word. The Arian conflict at Nicaea comes down to a single letter in a word, *homoousios* or *homoiousios*. The former states that God and Jesus are exactly the *same* in substance and the latter that they are only *similar* in substance. Most Arians could accept the latter but not the former.

Arius is not a bishop and cannot vote unless he can obtain sufficient support to become a bishop. However, he has the support of several powerful bishops, including Eusebius of Caesarea and Eusebius of Nicomedia, both of whom are close to Constantine.

Meletius and His Supporters

The issue for this group is what to do with the apostate, those who were not faithful under persecution. These are people who sacrificed to the Roman gods to avoid martyrdom. Meletius believed that only after a substantial period of observation to confirm their continued faithfulness should these apostate Christians be allowed to return to the Church. He also did not believe any should ever be allowed to return to the clergy.

There is a complex history behind this controversy in Egypt that goes back to the persecution of around 303 C.E. Peter, bishop of Alexandria, and Meletius, bishop of Lycopolis, the second major city of Egypt, were in prison together along with a number of subordinate bishops. The more important bishops were being saved for execution on a special occasion, so they were in prison for an extended time. A number of imprisoned clergy and lay people avoided martyrdom by making sacrifices to the Roman gods. Members of this group approached Peter and Meletius and asked to do penance and to be allowed to return to the faith and to their positions in the clergy. Meletius and the majority of those in prison had little sympathy for this request and refused to accept them. They felt it made a mockery of those who were already martyrs. Peter took the opposite view. He felt penance was sufficient and that it was best to have these people back inside the Church instead of allowing them to drift away from their faith.

Meletius and Peter argued bitterly over this issue, and Peter eventually hung a cloth across the prison and asked his supporters to come to his side and those of Meletius to stay on the other side. The two sides refused to talk to each other and began to hold separate worship services. Meletius called his group the Church of the Martyrs.

Eventually, Peter was beheaded, but some of his followers were released. Meletius and others were sent into exile to work in the salt mines. As Meletius traveled into exile, he ordained many clergy and bishops and established churches.

When Meletius was released from exile, he went to Alexandria, where he was received by the two leading deacons who were not in prison, one of whom was Arius. Meletius excommunicated two leaders appointed by Peter and began to consecrate priests and bishops to fill open seats. Meletius ultimately consecrated 29 bishops who were in conflict with Peter and his successors. After Peter of Alexandria was martyred, Achillas and then Alexander took over as metropolitan of Alexandria. Alexander then consecrated his own bishops to fill positions already filled by Meletius. This led to open fighting between the two groups.

Ultimately, Meletius's Church of the Martyrs had churches throughout Egypt and Palestine, with bishops and priests he had ordained. Meletius claimed some of the same church property for his church that had been claimed by Alexander.

The Council of Nicaea must sort out this conflict and restore peace in Egypt if the Church is to be unified and peaceful. Thus, Constantine will insist that some resolution be found to bring this conflict to an end.

Followers of Valentinus

Valentinus (c.100–c.160 C.E.) was the author of a Gnostic text known as the "Gospel of Truth" and was the leader of a group of Gnostics who believed that Jesus did not become divine until his baptism, when he was united with a divine being (or Aeon) to become Christ. Before that, he was a human being. In this respect, these Gnostics are aligned with Arius. Jesus was born of the biological union of Mary and Joseph. He may even have been married to Mary Magdalene, though this would have been a minority view even among this group. The role of Jesus, once united with the divine reality, was to bring divine knowledge to humankind. Jesus shared this knowledge with his disciples after his resurrection, and through it the disciples became like Jesus, able to do miracles and raise the dead. This knowledge was available only to the most devout believers, and through it they could become like Jesus. The Church was entrusted with knowledge, and it was contained in secret writings (The Secret Book of John, etc.). Once learned, the secret knowledge would allow any believer to become one with God and to have all of the powers that Jesus displayed. Numerous passages in the New Testament attest to Jesus's belief that his disciples would have the same powers he did (see John 14:12), and the apostles in fact are reported to have had such powers (see Acts 5:17–19 for one example).

In their search for knowledge and wisdom, Gnostics did not restrict themselves to Christian writings. They also had access to Plato's writings and to the entire range of current religious and philosophical thought. Students in Gnostic roles may use any of these writings in formulating their positions. Gnostics were much more universal in their beliefs and did not restrict the operation of the Word and of wisdom to Jesus or the Jewish writers. Wisdom is found throughout human experience. In fact, some Gnostics believed that Yahweh, the God of the Jews, was actually an evil entity and that the true God of Jesus was a higher God who had nothing to do with the material world. They saw knowledge as a way to free them from the bondage of the creation and allow them to return to a higher spiritual plane, from which they had been torn at the creation of the world.

The way to knowledge of God was primarily through mystical experiences, and the Valentineans were primarily ascetics who lived monastic lives and spent their time in meditation as a means of self-knowledge. The Buddhist practice of meditation and the quest for Enlightenment may be the clearest modern analogues of this type of practice. The Gnostic approach was a very personal quest and did not require the mediation of priests or bishops between the Christian and God. Although some Christians might have more experience or clearer knowledge than others, all spiritual experiences were between the person and God. To the extent that Gnostic sects were organized at all, they were very open and democratic. Bishops were elected frequently, on a rotating basis, and there is some evidence that women were elected bishops from time to time since the physicality of their bodies was no hindrance to their power given that bodies were not that important to spiritual truth.

The Gnostics believed that baptism by water was only the first level of initiation for Christians and that it offered no guarantee of salvation (see the Gospel of Philip and also Pagels 2003, p. 136). They had a higher level of initiation, but the nature of these mysteries is lost; possibly, it was considered too secret to ever be written down. However, initiates at the highest level were considered "Christs" and were reported to raise the dead and perform other miracles. They were considered to have died to their bodies and to have been spiritually raised from the dead as Jesus had been.

The followers of Valentinus saw the existence of a large Church, which only initiated believers into the first level of the faith, as a good and necessary thing. Thus, they often worked to find compromise between the more radical elements of the factions at the same time as they worked to initiate more Christians into the deeper mysteries of the faith. Some traditional bishops are known to have attended Gnostic services, and it is possible that some bishops in the Nicaea game have been secretly initiated into high levels of the Gnostic sect and do not wish this fact to be known.

Followers of Paul of Samosata

Paul of Samosata (200–275 C.E.) represented a particularly interesting case. He believed that Jesus was the "adopted" Son of God, having been chosen at his baptism. Thus, he is rather more extreme than the Arians in his view of the relationship of Jesus to God.

A number of charges were made against Paul of Samosata. He was accused of using his position as bishop to amass a personal fortune. He lived in a house with several beautiful women who claimed to be his celibate companions. He engaged in a very flamboyant style of worship service. Applause was encouraged. He had women dancing and singing in his services. He walked around town with his female companions. In general, he did not seem to present the kind of image that the Church wished to project. His main offense, however, was that he espoused the theology that would come to be identified as Arian. He was discredited more than 50 years before the Council of Nicaea and was stripped of his position as bishop of Antioch. Some churches associated with Paul of Samosata still followed his style of worship, including allowing participation of women and a flamboyant worship style. His followers claimed that some of the charges against him had been fabricated to help discredit his theology.

Ebionites and Marcionites

These polar opposite positions have been discussed previously. The Ebionites were Jewish Christians, and the Marcionites were intent on removing all traces of Jewish influence. It is improbable that by the time of the Council of Nicaea there were any bishops who would have been identified as adherents to the more extreme versions of these two ideologies. However, the tension between these two polar opposites was still very much evident in issues such as the proper date of Easter. It is therefore useful for students to be familiar with these positions, and some roles have aspects of these positions built into them.

Docetists

Docetist (do-CET-ist) Christians questioned how it was possible for God to die. If Jesus was in fact God incarnate, then how could God die on a cross? If God did not die, then how could there be a resurrection? These questions got them in lots of trouble since the bodily resurrection of Jesus was a central belief for most Christians. From the earliest times, many Christian writings (both canonical and noncanonical), such as those of Clement and Ignatius, constantly attacked the Docetist position. Gnostics often suggested that Jesus either did not die at all or that the Christ part of Jesus left him before his death. All of these questions and explanations were attempts to deal with the logical impossibility of the omnipotent God dying.

Docetists are not really a faction, but Docetism is an important idea that relates to the Gnostic position in terms of a fundamental dualism between spirit and matter. It is an important word to understand in reading early writings. Many at Nicaea would have considered this a dangerous heresy that a creed must eliminate from the Church.

Donatists

Donatus (b.?–355 C.E.) was a bishop in the region of Carthage in North Africa who believed that any priest or bishop who had betrayed the faith during the Great Persecution (becoming a *traditore*, or traitor) had to be rebaptized and reordained in order to regain his authority to celebrate the sacraments and perform other priestly or episcopal duties. Donatism was a movement within the emerging Christian churches following the years of persecution and martyrdom around the beginning of the fourth century. Donatists did not believe that sacraments performed by apostate clergy were valid. The opponents of Donatism argued that making the validity of the sacraments depend on the moral worthiness of the priest would make it impossible for a person receiving the sacrament to know whether it had been validly consecrated. No one can fully know the inner moral worthiness of someone else, making reception of the sacrament uncertain and possibly endangering the soul of the recipient.

3

The Game

Fundamental Conflict and the Role of Constantine

The major issue that led Constantine to call the Council of Nicaea was the Arian controversy. Within this game, Constantine has convened the council but has taken no power himself within the proceedings. He sees the bishops as the authority on spiritual issues. His goal is to ensure an outcome that meets his goal of Christian unity. Constantine will open the council and may speak at any time he wishes, though he will normally ask permission from the presiding bishop before doing so. But everyone knows his power and has no illusions to the contrary. Constantine does not vote and cannot excommunicate bishops or rule on theological matters.

Constantine has the entire resources of the Roman Empire at his disposal, and this gives him great power for behind-the-scenes activity in Nicaea. If Constantine particularly likes the statements of a bishop, he is in the position to grant that bishop special favors. This could be money to build a cathedral in the bishop's major city, or it could be money for the bishop to support widows and orphans. Alternatively, the bishop could use the gifts of the emperor for more personal use, to build a palace or to live in luxury. In general, Constantine will grant one such favor (called an *Imperial Boon*) to a participant in the council at the beginning of the second through the sixth game sessions. This will be based on the emperor's judgment of who has made the best presentation supporting his goal of Christian unity.

Constantine also has the power of life or death over every person in the empire. He has not shown any inclination to use this power recklessly or casually. In cases where he wished to have opponents eliminated from the scene, he has normally found ways to bring criminal charges against them, though in the case of his wife, he appears to have organized an apparent or forced suicide. If Constantine finds any bishop at the council to be

41

obstructing his goals too forcefully, he has the option of removing that bishop. If Constantine chooses to have anyone executed, the council can discuss the propriety of his actions and may censure him if it wishes to do so. The consequences of such a vote are not clear, but Constantine needs the bishops to support his personal goals, and this gives the council at least a small amount of power. Thus, Constantine's absolute power is limited by his own goals of building unity. If he were to attempt to exercise theological power, the bishops might even decide to end the council, thus dooming Constantine's goal of Christian unity.

The first issue before the council is to write a creed that can gain majority support. Once this creed is written, all bishops must sign it and attest publicly to their acceptance of it. Those who do not agree lose their vote in the council. During the council debates after the creed is approved, it is possible for the creed to be modified in any game session. However, if it is modified, all bishops must again subscribe to the modified version. Only those bishops who subscribe to the new version will be allowed to vote. Those who do not accept the modifications will lose their votes, and any who formerly lost their votes but who accept the new creed regain their votes.

Issues to Be Decided

The major issues for debate at Nicaea are described in this section, with some background on each. There are additional issues that may be brought to the council that are not included in this list. These are related in some way to the major issues discussed here.

As you approach your opponents in the discussion of these issues, you should assume that all bishops, including yourself, are sincere in their beliefs. Until very recently, Christians could be executed just for openly acknowledging their faith. Many bishops bear the scars of torture and imprisonment. Their beliefs are deeply held. On each of these issues, the bishops on opposite sides believe that they are correct. If you disagree, you need to

present a convincing argument based on the scriptures and the traditions of the Church. On issues of theology, bishops are all firm in their belief that their way represents the truth they find in the writings of the apostles. On issues of church organization, the differences relate to varying ideas about how to build the strongest organization and how to remain true to the traditions of the past 300 years of the Church. Although bishops are human and people are susceptible to all the normal desires for power, control, and status, there are reasons why each position could be the way to build a strong Church that will follow the Great Commission of Jesus to

> go and make disciples of all nations, baptizing them in the name of the Father and of the Son and of the Holy Spirit, and teaching them to obey everything I have commanded you. And surely I am with you always, to the very end of the age. (Matt. 28:19–20)

WRITE A CREED THAT DESCRIBES WHAT CHRISTIANS BELIEVE TO ACHIEVE A UNIVERSAL CHURCH

For centuries, Christians have intoned the words "in the name of the Father, and the Son, and the Holy Spirit" in baptism and Communion. The problem to be decided by the council is the nature of the relationship between these "persons" of God. A creed should include statements about the nature of each and the relationship between them. The most contentious issue is the fact that the Arian and Alexandrian views on this issue are difficult to reconcile. There may also be some differences of opinion on how to describe the Father and the Holy Spirit in the creed.

What Is the Relationship between God and Jesus?

What is the nature of God? Can a transcendent God have any direct contact at all with humanity and the world? Is Jesus of the same substance as God the Father, or is he different from the Father in some essential way? Was there a time before which Jesus the Son did not exist? Did the Son exist before he was born in the flesh? Was the Son created? Is the Son changeable in any way? Is God divisible, as when the Son was begotten?

Arius and his followers take a view that is very different from the canonical view that emerged from the Council of Nicaea—that God is one being who is experienced in three different ways: Father, Son, and Holy Spirit. These are coeternal, coequal, and represent only different manifestations of God.

The Gnostics have yet a different view. The council needs to settle this issue once and for all and eliminate the distractions of the ongoing debate.

Arius and his followers will probably accept the Apostles' Creed, already discussed. Those who wish to purge Arians and their ideas from the Church will need to find language that makes the equality of God and Jesus more specific.

ISSUES OF CHURCH ORGANIZATION

Now that the Church is a recognized religion, there are a number of organizational issues that need to be settled. If the Christian church is to be universal, with a unified set of beliefs and a growing membership, these issues need to be decided.

What Is the Relative Role of the Metropolitan Bishops?

During the past century, metropolitan bishops such as those in Alexandria, Antioch, Caesarea, and Rome have had authority over all other bishops in their regions. The bishop of Alexandria controlled all of northern Africa, the bishop of Rome controlled Italy, the bishop of Caesarea controlled Palestine, and so forth. These bishops claim a direct lineage of ordination to one of the twelve apostles of Jesus, and they use this as their source of authority (Eusebius, *The History of the Church*, book III, chapter 4, and book V, chapters 6 and 12). More recently, this system has been broken up, and the power of these regional leaders has diminished. The metropolitan bishops would like to regain their authority, and the local bishops will

generally oppose this loss of power. At stake is the overall structure of the emerging Church, which will also have an impact on its ability to maintain a consistent theology. Will there be a democracy with all bishops essentially equal, or will there be a hierarchy in which power is concentrated in the hands of a few? The model of the Roman Empire may prevail. Emperor Diocletian reorganized the Roman bureaucracy into a strong hierarchy, and this is the prevailing organizational model. But local authorities will fight for all the power they can get. There are special problems in Africa, where Alexander of Alexandria claims to be metropolitan of all Africa. If the council endorses this, there is a possibility of splitting the Church, with Meletius and the Novatianists leaving altogether.

If the council were to vote that metropolitan bishops hold power in their regions, the other organizational question is whether all metropolitans are equal or if one is the head of the Church, with the others subordinate to him. If all metropolitans are equal, then some mechanism will be needed for them to resolve regional differences. This could be accomplished by occasional meetings. If the council were to decide that the Church needed a single primary leader, then the question of which metropolitan should hold this role would need to be decided.

Which Metropolitan Bishop Has Power in Palestine?

Since the destruction of Jerusalem in 70 C.E., the bishop of Caesarea (where Eusebius is now bishop) has been the metropolitan of all Palestine. However, the bishop of Jerusalem, site of the crucifixion and resurrection and where the leaders of the Christian church lived during its early history, believes that he should have spiritual primacy as well as jurisdictional authority over Palestine. Caesarea was the seat of Roman power in Palestine, but it has no real tradition of spiritual authority in the Church. The history of Jerusalem as a center of spiritual power can be traced to Genesis, when

Abraham went to Salem (Jerusalem) to make offerings of thanksgiving (Gen. 14:18–20). This is a personal issue for the two major bishops and their supporters. It doesn't matter much to anyone else, but everyone should consider the symbolic and practical arguments in reaching a decision.

What Will Be the Powers of Future Church Councils?

Whether this issue arises depends in part on the decision about metropolitan bishops. If metropolitans are given great power and a strong hierarchy is established, then the need for future Church councils will be minimal, though the Council of Nicaea might decide to make metropolitans subject to future councils. On the other hand, if all bishops are equal, there may need to be a mechanism to settle major disputes. Canons regarding future councils should wait until the power of metropolitans has been determined.

What Are the Qualifications for Ordination and Promotion of Clergy?

A related concern is that ordination into the clergy and promotion to higher ranks may become political as well. Should clergy be well schooled in the scriptures and doctrines of the Church before ordination? Clearly, it would not be politically wise for anyone at the Council of Nicaea to accuse another bishop of political appointments to the clergy, but this is a fear that many have in the current climate of rapid growth of the Church in both size and wealth. Should there be educational requirements or waiting periods between baptism into the Church and ordination into the clergy? Should clergy be required to wait before being promoted to bishop?

What Is the Role of Celibacy in the Clergy?

There are a number of issues related to sexuality that may arise at the council. There is a growing movement in some quarters to replace martyrdom with chastity as a sign of devotion to God. Particularly in Egypt, but increasingly throughout the Church, there are communities of believers who set themselves apart from the world to live in poverty and chastity. Is this something to be valued, is it neutral, or is it detrimental to the faith?

The issue of celibacy for priests and bishops will definitely need to be addressed by the council. It is traditional in much of the empire for priests and bishops not to marry, because sexual relations are believed by many to distract people from a higher, spiritual life. However, what should someone do who is already married when he is ordained? Can he continue to have intercourse with his wife, or must he become celibate after ordination? Does the demand of celibacy place too much temptation on priests? Some may even suspect that the demand for celibacy is designed to prevent the birth of children who would have a hereditary claim to Church property or rank. If this is the rationale for celibacy, is intercourse outside marriage (with concubines or prostitutes) acceptable? Constantine has very strong feelings on this issue, which the council will need to consider.

A careful reading of the Church's early history in Eusebius's *History of the Church* may be helpful in addressing some aspects of this question. Were any of the 12 apostles married? Did they have children?

The issue of what to do about the followers of Paul of Samosata also is indicative of the problems that can occur when clergy keep women in their house other than a mother, sister, or aunt. This is common in some regions and forbidden in others. Does the presence of members of the opposite gender place too much temptation on the clergy and those who live with them? Does the appearance of impropriety in itself constitute reason enough to prohibit this practice?

Matthew 19:12 reads, "For there are eunuchs who have been so from birth, and there are eunuchs who have been made eunuchs by men, and there are eunuchs who have made themselves eunuchs for the sake of the kingdom of heaven. He who is able to receive this, let him receive it." One bishop read this literally and therefore castrated himself. After this, he had a woman who was not his relative living with him in his house. Is this an example of extreme faith that should be encouraged or a perversion that should be punished?

DATES FOR IMPORTANT RELIGIOUS HOLIDAYS

What Is the Proper Date to Celebrate the Resurrection?

At the time of the Council of Nicaea, the feast to celebrate the Death and Resurrection of Jesus was called by the Greek term Pascha, referring to Passover.[1] At first, the Church followed the Jewish calendar, beginning the celebration on Nissan 14. Most Christians fasted for three days and held a vigil on the third night. This was followed by the Feast of the Resurrection on the fourth day. This was based on the understanding that Jesus instituted the sacrament of Communion on the first night of Passover, was crucified the following day, and remained in the grave until the third day, when he rose from the dead. There were conflicts within the Christian community because many wanted to celebrate the Resurrection on Sunday every year, but Nissan 14 moved through the week each year. Considerable debate had occurred about this feast in the centuries before the council. In 190 C.E., Bishop Victor of Rome tried to force all churches to celebrate Pascha on the Sunday after Passover. This was met with strong opposition from those who wanted to keep it linked directly to Passover.

Students need to understand that there is a symbolic connection between Jesus's death and the killing of the Paschal lamb at Passover. Read Exodus 12 for background on Passover, and search for scripture passages in the New Testament that reference the Paschal lamb for more background. The Easter Vigil service of the Church is another possible keyword to obtain information. An early discussion of the meaning of Jesus's death can be found in writings of Bishop Melito of Sardis (c.170 C.E.), which can be found at http://www.kerux.com/doc/0401A1.asp. His writings led ultimately to the doctrine of Original Sin, which persists in the Church today. This recently discovered text was widely circulated and was translated into many languages (Chadwick 1979, p. 85).

By the time of the Council of Nicaea, the lunar calendar of the Jews was applied in at least two ways to determine when to celebrate the Resurrection. In Alexandria and Rome, the rule was that the Resurrection should be celebrated on the Sunday following the fourteenth day after the first new moon after the spring equinox. In part of Asia Minor, including Antioch and Syria, the calculation was made based on the actual Jewish calendar, and there was the possibility of the Resurrection being before or after the equinox. There is already general agreement that the entire universal church should have a single day for the celebration. But what day should that be? Should the Jews be consulted? Should the Alexandrian and Roman interpretation of the Jewish lunar calendar be preserved? Or should a single Sunday in the Roman calendar be used to completely divorce the most important day of the Christian year from everything Jewish? Constantine is clearly interested in removing Jewish connections from the Church.

Constantine's opinion on this topic can be presumed from a letter he wrote on the subject after the Council of Nicaea:

It appeared an unworthy thing that in the celebration of this most holy feast we should follow the practice of the Jews, who have impiously defiled their hands with enormous sin, and are, therefore, deservedly afflicted with blindness of soul. For we have it in our power, if we abandon their custom, to prolong the due observance of this ordinance to future ages, by a truer order, which we have preserved from the very day of the passion until the present time. Let us then have nothing in common with the detestable Jewish crowd; for we have received from our Saviour a different way. . . . Beloved brethren, let us with one consent adopt this course, and withdraw ourselves from all participation in their baseness. For their boast is absurd indeed, that it is not in our power without instruction from them to observe these things. . . . Hence it is that on this point as well as others they have no perception of the truth, so that, being altogether ignorant of the true adjustment of this question, they sometimes celebrate Easter twice in the same year. Why then should we follow those who are confessedly in grievous error?[2]

There are several options for resolving this issue:

1. Use the Sunday closest to the spring equinox (March 21 in the Roman calendar) for Resurrection Sunday. This will align Resurrection Sunday with the spring fertility rites celebrated in many parts of the empire. In Britain, these are dedicated to the fertility goddess Ēostre. It can be presumed that this outcome would be favored by Constantine. Virtually every part of the empire already has a feast around the spring equinox to celebrate the rebirth of the earth after the winter. Moving the celebration of the Resurrection to this period would aid in converting the pagans to Christianity and avoid adding another feast that occurs at confusing times. The pagans would come to celebrate the rebirth of Jesus instead of a feast honoring their local fertility goddesses. Constantine would also like to have a celebration of Jesus's birth during the winter solstice holiday of Saturnalia, held around modern December 21. Saturnalia celebrates the birth of the Sun God, widely considered the Supreme God by Constantine and the cult of Mithras. Since Constantine equates the Supreme God with the God of Jesus, this makes logical sense as the date to celebrate Jesus's birth.

    This choice of the spring equinox to celebrate the Resurrection may also be favored by those who wish to purge residual Jewish character from the Church. The difficulty of determining the date of Passover each year, and the requirement that the people doing it must both observe the moon and understand the Jewish calendar, make a fixed date very appealing to Constantine and many other bishops. They feel that the complexity of the Jewish calendar (see appendix 2) is daunting and unnecessary for Christians. Some object strongly that they have to consult Jewish authorities every year to set the date of the most important Christian feast.

2. Follow the lunar calendar of the Jews and make the Resurrection celebration the first Sunday after the start of Passover. There are both theological and practical reasons for this choice. The theology of the Church is that Jesus was sacrificed for our sins in a direct parallel to the killing of the Passover lamb by Moses. The blood of that lamb was sprinkled on the doorposts of Jewish homes so that the Angel of Death would "pass over" them and leave their firstborn sons alive. The blood of Jesus serves this function and causes God to forgo the sentence of death placed on all children of Adam and Eve in the Garden of Eden. This provides the theological underpinning coordinating the celebration of the Resurrection with Passover. Students supporting this position will want to research this in more detail so they can make a thorough argument. Also, if the determination of the holiday is very complicated, it will give authority to the bishops who will have to announce the date each year.

3. The lunar calendar as employed in Alexandria and Rome could be used. In this system, the Resurrection is celebrated on the Sunday following the fourteenth day after the first new moon after the spring equinox. Those who support this approach believe it

retains the connection to Passover while eliminating the possibility of two Resurrection celebrations in one year. This is seen as a "corrected" version of the lunar calendar approach. Because there is some conflict within the empire over the date of the equinox, it will probably be necessary to pick one metropolitan to maintain the observations and announce the date each year. Rome and Alexandria are the obvious contenders for this role.

Students should see appendix 2 for a detailed discussion of the details of the Roman and Jewish calendars that form the basis of this issue.

What Is the Proper Date to Celebrate the Birth of Jesus?

The council may also consider whether to celebrate the birth of Jesus and when, though this is a minor matter for most bishops.

ISSUES OF PARTICIPATION IN THE CHURCH BY SPECIAL GROUPS

One reason Constantine called this council was to deal with the controversies that arose during the Great Persecution over whether people were faithful or not. This led to deep divisions in churches, especially in North Africa. There are other regional groups, such as the followers of Paul of Samosata, who have practices that place them at odds with others in the Church. There are also people clamoring to join the Church who some suspect are not true believers now that membership is favored by the emperor, and some wish to ensure the purity of the faithful. Finally, there are some areas where women have participated in worship in various leadership roles. What is the proper role of women in the Church?

What Should Be Done with Apostates, Those Who Succumbed to Persecution?

During the Great Persecution, some Christians, and even clergy, made sacrifices to the Roman gods, turned over scriptures to the authorities, and in other ways failed to maintain their faith. Some wish to forgive these people, referred to as "apostates." They would welcome these apostates back into their congregations immediately and even return them to their offices in the clergy. Others feel they should be punished in some way and be required to demonstrate their faith through some level of testing. This could involve instruction and a waiting period, possibly of several years, during which the individual would be observed to see if they maintained a Christian life. Only after proving their worthiness would they be allowed to return as full members and possibly resume offices they held. A few would even exclude these people from the Church forever or at least from the clergy.

What Should Be Done about the Novatianist Sect?

Acesius is a bishop of the Novatianist sect, a group of Christians in Libya who broke with the other Christians under the leadership of Bishop Cyprian more than 50 years before the Council of Nicaea. On general issues of doctrine, the Novatianists differ from the rest of the Church on issues of discipline. The original issue was what to do with Christians who could not stand up to the persecution and made sacrifices to the Roman gods or denied their faith. The Novatianists have very strict rules that do not allow these people to return to the Church now that persecution has ended. They take similarly strong positions on all weakness shown by supposed Christians.

Acesius is attending the council at the invitation of Constantine, who would like to see unity. It will be important to Constantine that this group return to communion with the universal church he envisions. If the council is not firm enough on issues of discipline, it is very likely that the Novatianists will go their separate way and remain as a separate group. This will be very disappointing to Constantine. The Novatianists may find common ground with Meletius, since his issue with Alexander also has its roots in the treatment of apostates.

If Alexander becomes metropolitan for all of Africa, there is a possibility that Acesius will abandon his efforts to purify the Roman church and leave the council.

What Should Be Done about Meletius and Those He Ordained?

Meletius of Lycopolis has founded his own church, the Church of the Martyrs, in direct competition with Peter of Alexandria. Alexander, who replaced Peter when he died, is asking the council to remove Meletius as bishop and remove all of those he has consecrated. The bishop of Alexandria has historically been metropolitan of all Egypt, and he wishes his control to include all of Africa. Meletius acted without the approval of Peter or his successors, who consider Meletius's church to be illegal.

If the council accepts Alexander's claim as Metropolitan with power over all of Egypt, then Meletius will certainly be removed and will lose his vote in the council. A decision would then also be needed regarding what to do with the priests and bishops Meletius has ordained. Can they keep their posts? Will they need to be rebaptized or reconsecrated by Alexander? Rebaptism would only be required if it were determined that the initial baptism into the faith was not a true baptism, since true baptism is considered by most to be irrevocable. But reconsecration to the priesthood or episcopate would certainly be reasonable in any case. If Meletius is allowed to remain as bishop of Lycopolis, what powers will he retain if Alexander is given full authority in all of Egypt? On the other hand, if Meletius prevails, then Alexander will lose considerable power, and control of Egypt will be divided between Alexandria and Lycopolis. Then a decision will be needed regarding the churches under direct contention. It may be necessary to build additional churches for the contending parishes, as Constantine has already done to settle a similar conflict in Libya.

If the council endorses a plan to place the metropolitan bishop of Alexandria in charge of the entire African church, this could spell disaster for

Meletius since Alexander may choose to excommunicate Meletius and those he ordained from the Church to end the quarrel with them over power in Egypt. The excommunication of Meletius will certainly destroy church unity since he will leave the Church and the council if excommunicated. This would be a major blow to Constantine's desire for a unified church.

What Should Be Done about Followers of the Ways of Paul of Samosata?

Paul was accused of many things (see appendix 1). He was removed as bishop of Antioch as a result of his belief that Jesus was born entirely human. After his removal one of his followers, Lucian of Antioch, founded a school for clergy that produced a group of students that included Arius, Eusebius of Nicomedia, Maris, Theodonis (also spelled Theogonis), and others. Their position on Jesus is much more moderate than that of Paul. Arius, Eusebius, and Theodonis have led exemplary lives, free of scandal. For purposes of this game, Maris and some of his associates are more flamboyant and charismatic leaders and have been accused of being close followers of Paul in many ways. Although claiming to be celibate, they also live with the women who accompany them in public. This has led to rumors of sexual impropriety. Paul and his followers also encourage women to participate in worship services, and the services are said to be rather flamboyant, with applause and cheering. Some feel that such behavior during worship is irreverent and turns what should be a time of worship into a carnival. Should the council set standards for clerical behavior that will keep the Church above reproach in all areas and assure that women play only their proper role? What is that role anyway? In what ways should Christian behavior differ from that of even virtuous pagans?

What Is the Process for Becoming a Member of the Church?

The rapid growth of the Church, now that it is popular, concerns some but not all bishops. They fear that many of the new converts are joining only to improve their chances for advancement in the government. Some would like to establish various stages of training before full membership in the Church. These would provide a barrier to casual membership now that Christians don't face the threat of death for their beliefs. On the other hand, there are ample examples in the scriptures that conversion to Christianity and acceptance of Jesus as Lord and Savior are all that are required for salvation. Does the Church want to put up barriers to membership if there are no such barriers to salvation?

What Is the Role of Women in the Church?

Clearly, women played a vital role during the first century of the Church. The apostle Paul speaks glowingly of the contributions they made to his ministry. There is some controversy over what his letters say about the role of women. Some of his letters place constraints on their participation, but some copies of the same letter offer different directions. It is not clear what the apostle Paul actually wrote. The Gnostics often grant women full equality in all things, including ordaining them as priests and bishops. No women have been invited to this council, and the Gnostics have been increasingly shunned by the majority of the Church over the past century. Still, the apostle Paul is quite clear that in Christ there are no differences between male and female. Does that apply to the Church as well?

Women played a variety of roles in the early church. From the earliest days of the first century, widows were supported by the Church. They gradually became organized into groups that prayed for church members, performed other duties of service to the poor, and other tasks. Women also served as deaconesses to provide service to the church members and clergy. By the fourth century, this had evolved into formal groups of widows and virgins who led monastic lives of service and prayer.

However, it is not clear that by the fourth century women were ordained as presbyteresses,

the equivalent of priests. Thus, women no longer play an active role in the worship service or as clergy of the Church. It is not clear when after the first century this change occurred. Paul of Samosata was condemned by many for having women participate actively in his church services as well as for his flamboyant style of worship. One can assume that some of the followers of Paul of Samosata still involve women as active participants in their worship services.

RULES AND PROCEDURES

First, each student is the leader of a small group of like-minded bishops. The entire group will tend to follow your lead and vote as you do, so in all issues that come before the council, you control all their votes. Minor bishops control 15 votes, and the four metropolitan bishops control 25 votes owing to their greater authority. (The number of followers may also vary with class size.) Your first objective is to inspire this group to continue to follow your lead. You can do this by speaking at each council session and by asking your opponents probing questions and speaking eloquently and with good authority on the issues you support. If a bishop fails to speak in two successive council sessions, some of his supporters will probably find others to lead them. Thus, the gamemaster may reduce this bishop's voting block by up to five votes. If he continues to fail to provide leadership, he may lose all of his followers and be reduced to a single vote.

Second, Constantine controls the wealth of the empire. He may choose to reward those who make outstanding contributions to the council with special powers or with resources to enlarge their ministry. These often take the form of Imperial Boons. You don't know the details of this, but you should do the best job you can in hopes of attracting Constantine's attention and furthering your career and the well-being of your parish. Bishops who receive an Imperial Boon will gain supporters in their voting block at the expense of the others. Acquiring a Boon could greatly increase your influence in the council votes. But you will run the risk of being seen as too eager for earthly preferment if you too readily accept or are believed by your fellow bishops to desire an Imperial Boon. Your moral reputation could be at stake here.

Each role includes personal objectives relevant to some of the issues just discussed. The individual role sheets detail them. You should listen carefully to the arguments of the parties and make a decision based on who is most convincing. The issues on which you are indeterminate also offer opportunities for political maneuvering. You are free to use these issues in bargains to meet your own objectives. You have no specific stake in the outcome of the issues not covered in your personal victory objectives, but you should not do anything that would be out of character. If the gamemaster finds you to be acting inconsistently or the other bishops accuse you of selling your vote for personal advantage, you may be stripped of your victory points by the gamemaster.

Unfortunately, you know very little about other bishops attending the council. You will have to determine who your potential allies are and who may be amenable to dealing with you through your interactions with them. Therefore, it will be good to get to know the other students' roles as quickly as possible. However, *you cannot ask others specifically what their victory objectives are or directly divulge your own*. You must learn about the other characters through discussion in character. You can certainly ask probing questions about the nature of Jesus, the date to celebrate the Resurrection, and other issues before the council.

ORGANIZATION OF THE COUNCIL AND SPECIAL POWERS

Constantine

Constantine has absolute power throughout the empire. He may exile or expel people from the empire or from church councils such as the one at Nicaea. Exile does not necessarily affect the status of the exiled person's Communion or rank within the Church. Constantine can even have someone killed, though he has a reputation for following a rigid code of conduct. It is very unlikely that he would kill anyone unless there is credible evidence that the person committed a crime.

Constantine has no official role in the council other than as an observer. Constantine does not have a vote, has no theological training, and has not been baptized as a Christian.

Constantine may not be removed by any actions. His rule is absolute. He is also well protected by the Imperial Guards.

Presiding Bishop

The presiding bishop will open each meeting as he sees fit. The council will provide due deference to Constantine. All should stand in his presence and bow when approaching him. Ossius will be presiding bishop at the opening session of the council. He may be replaced by majority vote at any time.

The presiding bishop will maintain good order in the council sessions and determine the rules of procedure. There were no Robert's Rules of Order in the fourth century. Commonsense rules of procedure should suffice. Discussion should focus on and be limited to the specific motion on the floor. Amendments to any motion may be proposed. If the person making the motion accepts the amendment, then no vote is required. Otherwise, the motion can be amended only by a majority vote.

The presiding bishop must announce the topics for debate during the sessions after the creed one week before the actual debate. Therefore, students should bring motions related to their victory objectives to the presiding bishop during the first two game sessions. The presiding bishop controls the agenda. Additional issues may be raised during the game, but students are not expected to write papers on issues not posted in advance.

Council Powers

The council bishops have the power to excommunicate anyone. (The excommunicated person is excluded from receiving Communion and all other rites of the Church. This is a powerful weapon since to be denied Communion is to be denied access to

God's grace and the protection of the Church.) A majority vote of the bishops in the council is necessary to excommunicate a bishop or non-bishop person at the council.

Gamemaster

All bishops are expected to participate actively in the discussions every day. The gamemaster will monitor participation and may reduce the number of votes of students who fail to participate in class. Since each bishop begins as a leader of a group of 15–25 bishops, the failure to provide leadership will cause these followers to take their votes to bishops who participate more actively.

Nicaea, like much of the ancient world, is susceptible to plagues of various types. Any student who misses a game session for any reason may be deemed by the gamemaster to have died. In these cases, the student will be assigned a new role. This may require the student to do additional research and writing.

Voting

Voting in the council will normally begin with a show of hands to determine if there is a consensus. If the outcome is not obvious, a roll call vote will be held to account for the different numbers of votes held by the metropolitan bishops.

Metropolitan bishops are revered and powerful, and they command the votes of many lesser bishops. They have 25 votes each. Other bishops are less well known and have 15 votes each. Deacons are not bishops and do not vote, but any deacon can be consecrated a bishop as described in the next section.

Consecrating New Bishops

Some people in attendance at the council are presbyters or deacons, ordained clergy who are not yet bishops. Presbyters and deacons may seek to be elevated to the position of bishop so they can vote in the game. During this time, the appointment of bishops was not completely formalized. In some areas, the appointments may have been made by the metropolitan bishop. However, often the local congregation was involved in selecting the person they felt had the strongest leadership. This was the case when Arius and Alexander were competing to be elected bishop of Alexandria. Alexander got more votes than Arius and became metropolitan.

Each bishop was responsible for the Church in a specific city or region. The term used to describe this was "see." Thus, each bishop was responsible for supervising everything within his see, including the presbyters and deacons who served under him.

During the game, any presbyter or deacon who acquires an Imperial Boon may be consecrated as bishop if he can find three bishops to perform the ceremony. The Imperial Boon is submitted to the gamemaster, and the three bishops perform a laying on of hands. The candidate kneels, and the three bishops place their hands on his head and name him bishop in the name of the Father, the Son, and the Holy Spirit. The new bishop acquires 15 votes in the council at this point. In reality, a bishop must be a bishop of a particular congregation. The new bishops consecrated at the council will be considered provisional bishops until they are assigned to and accepted by a local congregation within a see. This does not change their ability to vote and participate in the council.

SCHEDULE OF CLASSES

The game schedule that follows is provided as a general guide. Professors may modify this. The initial setup of the game may vary from one to two or more weeks to allow discussion of the original texts. This will depend on the goals and level of the course.

Game Setup Sessions

The following texts must be read before the beginning of the game. The instructor may give a quiz covering some or all of this material.

Read this book.

Read the Gospels of Matthew, Mark, Luke, and John, the Acts of the Apostles, Romans, and 1 Corinthians.

These are the major sources of authority for arguments about the nature of Jesus, though some of you may have additional documents you will wish to bring to the discussion.

Additional texts that professors may require are listed in part 5.

Read the Introduction and books I–III, IX, and X of Eusebius's *History of the Church*.

Game Session 1

Constantine will open the session and is widely expected to name Ossius as presiding bishop. Constantine will probably wish to make an opening speech. Bishops should stand and bow when Constantine enters. The presiding bishop should offer a prayer.

- Each bishop will present a petition or letter of grievance to the emperor. Each should state one or more issues that he wishes considered and his positions on those issues. These should be brief—no more than one page total.
- The first session should come to a conclusion on a statement on the nature of God the Father. If time permits, the discussion can begin on the statement about Jesus.

Game Session 2

- This session will address what is possibly the most contentious issue at the council, the nature of Jesus and his relationship to God. This is at the core of the Arian controversy. By the end of the session, a formal statement on Jesus should be approved.

Game Session 3

- This is the final session on the creed. If necessary, additional discussions on the nature of Jesus can be held. The final portion of the creed, related to the Holy Spirit, must be decided. Any other issues that the council feels must be in the creed should also be finalized. The creed will be finalized in the last game session, at which point all bishops

must attest to their belief or be excommunicated. The creed can be modified by council vote at any time up until the end of the final game session.

Game Session 4

- What is the proper date for celebrating the Resurrection? Other issues for discussion may be announced by Ossius during game session 2.

Game Session 5

- The role of metropolitan bishops in general will be the focus of this session. The controversy between Meletius and Alexander will also be considered. Other issues for discussion may be announced by Ossius during game session 3.

Game Session 6

- The specific issue or issues for discussion will be announced by Ossius during game session 4.
- A final vote on the creed as it stands at this point will be held. All bishops must sign the creed and swear to their acceptance of it. Those who do not will be excommunicated from the universal church.

Postmortem

At the completion of the game, winners and losers, the question of tolerance, and what really happened are discussed. (Suggested background reading is appendix 3 in this text—The Doctrine of the Trinity—and chapter 12 in Ehrman's *Lost Christianities*.)

WRITING ASSIGNMENTS

1. Each student should prepare a one-paragraph grievance or request to present to Constantine during the first game session. These should be related to your character and your objectives in the game.
2. Each student should write a paper on some

part of the creed. Factions may divide the various aspects of their position on the creed issues so that some students write on the issue of God the Father, some on the relationship of the Son to the Father, and some on the nature of the Holy Spirit. More emphasis will be required on the second of these issues since this is the most contentious point. This paper should constitute at least half of your assigned writing for the game. The instructor will set the expectations for this. Normally, a minimum of five to seven pages is required. Note that your argument should be based on scripture as much as possible. Writing a paper on some aspect of the creed should begin by devising a specific statement for inclusion in the creed and then supporting that statement using biblical references and other sources. Papers that make only general arguments without any specific language are generally not very strong.

Note that the positions taken by various characters in the game are not always precisely defined or distinguished from positions taken by other characters. The struggle to create a creed with a single set of coherent statements of faith brings into discussion multiple and often ambiguous notions that sometimes overlapped each other even while claiming to be distinct from each other. Do not expect the views presented at the council to be without ambiguity or to be so precisely articulated that they can easily be distinguished from rival views, except in the most general way. Nevertheless, it is important that your character carefully research the views of your likely opponents so that you know how to challenge and, hopefully, defeat them in debate.

3. Each student will write one or two additional papers for the final three game sessions. These will focus on the specific issues to be debated as announced by the presiding bishop. Since each student has multiple issues on which to build a winning strategy, the decision of which issues to write on will require coordination with others whom you identify as having similar objectives and also require an effort to do a thorough job on a few issues rather than just a quick look at all of them. As with the papers on the creed, you should begin the process of writing by drafting a short one- or two-sentence canon that can be voted on by the council and then build your paper around an argument for that statement.

Note that there is a difference between language that you intend to put into the creed articulating essential Christian beliefs and language that is more appropriate for the canons of the Church.

Canons are essentially laws and have to do with policies regarding the practices (not the core beliefs) of the Church. For example, there might be a canon stating the eligibility or noneligibility of women for the priesthood, setting forth the age at which someone can have voting rights in the Church, when the Resurrection of Jesus should be celebrated, what the power of metropolitan bishops should be, and so on. Canons are an excellent venue for determining the resolution of some of the more contentious issues before the council.

Statements in the creed take the form of "We believe . . . ." You can review various creeds of the Christian church at the online resource listed previously to see examples of creedal language. Creeds can be political in what they select to include and omit.

4

Roles and Factions

In the discussion that follows, the names of metropolitan bishops appear **boldfaced**, and these bishops initially cast 25 votes. The names of nonvoting characters appear in *italics*. The names of all other bishops are set in roman type, and these bishops initially cast 15 votes. Not all of the bishops listed may be in attendance at the council.

Constantine—Augustus of Roman Empire. Constantine has no vote in the council and should seek permission from the presiding bishop to speak.

Alexandrian Faction. The term proto-orthodox is used here to indicate that this faction supports the complete equality of Jesus and God, which emerged historically as the position of the Church. On other issues, they may not agree.

Ossius (also spelled Hossius), bishop of Cordoba (Spain). Ossius is the presiding bishop. He has been a close advisor to Constantine for almost 20 years and is known to be opposed to Arius. Although he is a favorite of Constantine, he is, as a bishop, subject to majority vote by the other bishops at the council and can be removed by such a vote if he displeases them. Of course, his removal would greatly displease Constantine, and its ramifications would need to be carefully considered by the other bishops before attempting such a step.

Vito, representing Sylvester, bishop of Rome. Vito is a presbyter but speaks for the bishop, who claims Rome is the highest seat of the Church. He carries Sylvester's ring and has his full authority. He votes for Sylvester.

Alexander, bishop of Alexandria. He is a leading anti-Arian and claims to have authority over all of Egypt and Africa.

Athanasius. He is a presbyter and therefore not a voting member. He is assistant to Alexander of Alexandria. He is possibly too young to be a bishop (this is a matter of some contention) but is clearly going to succeed Alexander. He is rumored to be both ruthless and ambitious, as well as a brilliant speaker and writer.

Eustathius, bishop of Antioch. He was recently appointed to the second largest bishopric in Christendom and is a very strong opponent of Arius. He has refused to allow anyone who supports Arius's theology to work as clergy in Antioch.

Puritanus, a bishop from Acryla. He is thought to have very strict views on martyrdom and the treatment of apostates.

Acesius, bishop of Libya. He is the leader of the Novatianist sect.

Caecilianus, bishop of Carthage (Libya). He has been at the center of the conflict over who is the rightful bishop of Libya, which has troubled Constantine for more than a decade. Constantine is rightfully disgusted with his petty squabbling.

Nicholas, bishop of Myra (Asia Minor). He is noted for his generosity to the poor and to children. He is very strongly opposed to Arius.

Arian faction. All members of this group share the idea that Jesus was not identical in all ways with God. They may not agree on the details of the difference. On other issues, they may or may not agree.

Eusebius, bishop of Caesarea. He is under conditional excommunication from the Council of Antioch for his support of Arius. He is possibly the most distinguished scholar of scripture at the council. He is the metropolitan of all Palestine.

Eusebius, bishop of Nicomedia. He was an early supporter and friend of Arius. He is from the town where Constantine lives and that is the seat of imperial power. He is also very politically astute and did not attend the Council of Antioch, which he rightly

believed was stacked with opponents of Arius. He hopes for a better outcome at Nicaea and will work to ensure his continued position as bishop of the center of imperial power.

Arius. He is leader of the Arian faction and is under order of excommunication by Alexander of Alexandria. He is a noted preacher who often writes his sermons in verse and sings or chants them instead of speaking them. He is known to be very persuasive and popular. Arius is not a bishop at the start of the council and cannot vote.

Maris, bishop of Samosata. He is a follower of Paul of Samosata and can be assumed to support his practices.

Jacob, bishop of Palmyra (Syria). This bishop is thought to still follow many practices of the Torah law. He is reported to have submitted a list of dietary preferences for meals at the council.

Secundus, a bishop from Asia Minor. He is a close colleague of Eusebius of Caesarea.

Acacius, bishop of Ravenna (Northeastern Italy). Little is known about this bishop.

Theodonus, a bishop from Asia Minor. He is a close colleague of Eusebius of Caesarea and is under conditional excommunication for supposed Arian views.

Narcissus, a bishop from Spain. He is a close colleague of Eusebius of Caesarea and is under conditional excommunication for supposed Arian views.

Scotinus, bishop of Galatian Acyra. Little is known about this bishop.

Aelius, bishop of Sicilia. Little is known about this bishop.

Indeterminates. This group's position on the nature of Jesus and other issues is unknown.

Meletius, bishop of Lycopolis. He and Arius have supported each other against Alexander, though Meletius's theological position is unclear. Meletius's followers have clashed repeatedly and violently with the followers of Alexander over who controls churches and appoints certain bishops.

Sethius, bishop of Memphis (Egypt). Little is known about this bishop.

Augustin, bishop of Arelate (Gaul). Little is known about this bishop. He represents the major city of Gaul and seeks to be metropolitan of Gaul and Western Europe.

Marcus, bishop of Sinope. Rumors abound about the theology of this bishop, but little is known about him or his church.

Theclus. He is a presbyter and is the assistant to an unidentified bishop. He is known to be quite well read in the scriptures. He does not have a vote in the council but is allowed to speak.

Marcarius, bishop of Jerusalem. His position on Arius is unknown, but he is eager to have Jerusalem return to its position as the center of Christianity in Palestine.

Verus, bishop of Thessaly. Little is known about this bishop.

Ursacius, bishop of Singidunum (now Belgrade). Little is known about this bishop, but he is thought to be moderate.

Hieracas, bishop of Leontopolis. Little is known about this bishop.

Caelius, bishop of Sardinia. Little is known about this bishop.

Zopyrus, bishop of Libya Pentapolis. Little is known about this bishop from northern Africa.

FACTIONS

This game has clear factions on the main issue, the relationship of Jesus the Son to God the Father. One faction consists of Arius and those who agree with his theology. They are opposed by those who see God and Jesus as two manifestations of the same entity. The term *Alexandrian* is used to describe the second faction because Alexander is a leader of this faction. The students not in one of these factions can be considered indeterminates on the issues in the creed; however, not all are true indeterminates in that some of them may hold theological positions that are different from those of both the Arian and Alexandrian factions. The indeterminates may also have strong victory objectives that align with a faction on secondary issues.

The factions become somewhat less rigid on issues after the completion of the creed. Students will need to get to know all of the students in the class and explore their positions on the other issues during faction meetings and outside class to build coalitions of similar-minded students on the other issues.

5
Core Texts

ORIGINAL DOCUMENTS CONTEMPORANEOUS WITH THE COUNCIL OF NICAEA

The Holy Bible.

Eusebius, *The History of the Church*. London: Penguin Classics, 1965. Online at http://www.newadvent.org/fathers/2501.htm.

The online version of this text contains links to the relevant scriptures, definitions, and other material and is an excellent way for students to approach the arguments in the game.

Fourth Century Christianity web site. This site has a comprehensive collection of original sources related to this period. http://www.fourthcentury.com/.

The Letter of the Council of Antioch is an excellent contemporaneous statement of the orthodox position. It includes a creed written just before the Council of Nicaea. It is also the first known document in which a council pronounces anathemas against false doctrine. http://www.fourthcentury.com/council-of-antioch-ad-325/.

Documents on the Arian controversy. http://www.fourthcentury.com/urkunde-chart-opitz/. Documents concerning Meletius and his conflict with Alexander. http://www.fourthcentury.com/documents-concerning-the-meletian-schism/.

The Gnosis Archive. Ancient documents from Nag Hammadi. http://www.gnosis.org/naghamm/nhl.html.

Library of Early Christian Writings. http://www.earlychristianwritings.com/.

The Orthodox Christian Page. Detailed accusations against Paul of Samosata are contained in this early document: http://www.ocf.org/OrthodoxPage/reading/St.Pachomius/HE7_30.html.

SUPPLEMENTAL HISTORICAL RESOURCES ON CONSTANTINE AND NICAEA

Kousoulas, D. G. *The Life and Times of Constantine the Great*. Danbury, CT: Rutledge, 1997.

Rubenstein, R. E. *When Jesus Became God*. Orlando, FL: Harcourt, 1999.

Stephenson, Paul. *Constantine—Roman Emperor, Christian Victor*. New York: Overlook, 2010.

SUPPLEMENTAL RESOURCES ON EARLY CHRISTIANITY

Barnstone, William, and Marvin Meyer, eds. *The Gnostic Bible*. Boston: Shambhala, 2003.

Brown, Peter. *The Body and Society: Men, Women, and Sexual Renunciation in Early Christianity*, Twentieth Anniversary Edition with a New Introduction. New York: Columbia University Press, 2008.

Chadwick, Henry. *The Early Church*. New York: Dorset, 1986.

Crossan, John Dominic. *The Historical Jesus: The Life of a Mediterranean Jewish Peasant*. San Francisco: HarperOne, 1993.

———. *Jesus: A Revolutionary Biography*. San Francisco: HarperOne, 1994. Crossan is another respected scholar and writes very accessible books on Jesus.

Ehrman, Bart. *Lost Christianities*. New York: Oxford University Press, 2003. This book discusses the diversity of early Christian thought and the way texts were used to support the variety of beliefs. Some ideas from the book are summarized in the present volume, but the full text is useful for more in-depth research.

———. *Misquoting Jesus*. San Francisco: Harper, 2005. This book presents details on the use and misuse of texts to shape Christianity. Some ideas from the book are summarized in the present volume, but the full text is useful for more in-depth research.

———. *The New Testament: A Historical Introduction to the Early Christian Writings*. New York: Oxford University Press, 2003.

———. *The New Testament and Other Early Christian Writings: A Reader*. New York: Oxford University Press, 2003.

Ehrman, Bart, and Andrew S. Jacobs. *Christianity in Late Antiquity, 300–450 C.E.: A Reader*. New York: Oxford University Press, 2003.

Ferguson, Everett. *Backgrounds of Early Christianity*. Grand Rapids, MI: Eerdmans, 2003.

Fox, Robin Lane. *The Unauthorized Version: Truth and Fiction in the Bible*. New York: Knopf, 1992.

Frend, W. H. C. *The Rise of Christianity*. Philadelphia: Fortress Press, 1984.

Gonzalez, J. L. *Story of Christianity*, vol. 1. San Francisco: Harper and Row, 1984.

Hoffmann, R. J. *Celsus on the True Doctrine*. New York: Oxford University Press, 1987.

MacCulloch, Diarmaid. *Christianity—The First Three Thousand Years*. New York: Viking, 2009.

MacMullen, Ramsay. *Christianizing the Roman Empire: A.D. 100–400*. New Haven, CT: Yale University Press, 1984.

Pagels, Elaine. *The Gnostic Gospels*. New York: Vintage, 1989.

Sanders, E. P. *The Historical Figure of Jesus*. London: Penguin, 1993. This book presents a very readable review of what we know about Jesus and the sources available.

Acknowledgments

David E. Henderson

Frank Kirkpatrick and I express our gratitude to RTTP Editorial Board Editors John Eby and John Moser and to Development Editor Adam Porter for their contributions to improving this book. The many suggestions from users of this text are also appreciated.

I would first acknowledge my undergraduate professors at St. Andrews Presbyterian College who awakened a profound curiosity about how we went from the sayings of Jesus to the doctrines of the Church. I am also indebted to Elaine Pagels of Princeton University for her writings that introduced me to the Gnostic ideology. Most recently, I owe a debt to the works of Bart Ehrman, who has given me a much better grasp of the nature of the various nonorthodox versions of early Christianity and the way in which orthodoxy developed.

The roles in this game have been shaped by what I have read by these and other authors. The individuals cited bear no responsibility for the ways in which I have chosen to interpret their work. Bart Ehrman's delightful *Lost Christianities* has proved most useful in shaping the various positions for the roles.

My goal in writing this game was to allow students to internalize the vast diversity of early Christianity and to gain a sense of the process of going from this chaotic and violent time to the current state of orthodoxy. It is interesting to speculate on alternate histories that might have evolved if the decisions at Nicaea had been different. Both Prof. Pagels and Prof. Ehrman do this in their works. This game will allow students to shape the debates and engage firsthand in this speculation.

I also appreciate the willingness of Frank Kirkpatrick to join this effort as coauthor. Frank has brought his professional knowledge of early Christianity and Christian theology to this effort to ensure that my own efforts were corrected and expanded to fill the needs of the students.

I thank Mark Carnes, who has encouraged me to pursue this game, and I thank my wife, Susan, who has tolerated my frequent disappearances into the world of the third and fourth centuries.

Appendix 1. Introduction to Gnosticism

Frank Kirkpatrick

Gnosticism was a mode of thought that preceded the emergence of Christianity. Some form of it can be found in the mystical traditions of ancient Judaism as well as in modes of thought emanating from the works of Plato and the philosophies of what are called Middle-Platonism and Neo-Platonism. At the base of all these ways of thinking is a set of assumptions that would both attract many early Christian thinkers and, in some cases, repel them.

Gnosticism is best understood as a mode of thought, or type of thinking, rather than as a strict school, church, or clearly defined religion. At its heart is the assumption that there is a supreme, ultimate reality (God) whose nature is so far beyond the minds of human beings in the finite, empirical world that it cannot be disclosed or understood. The only access to the ultimate reality is through some kind of intermediary who reveals that ultimate reality. (The revelation is always obscured to some extent by the fact that it is received by beings whose nature is something other than the ultimate reality. The gap between the nature of God as God is in himself and the nature of human beings leads inevitably to the use of myths and allegories to convey the hidden mysteries of God.) But the vehicle of the revelation provides, in terms that the human recipient can grasp to some extent, a knowledge that will lift the recipient above his finite and limited condition and provide him access to the supreme mystery and through that access grant him "salvation." And that access is essentially through "knowledge," or in Greek, *gnosis*. The imparting of *gnosis*, the truth about the self's identity or kinship with ultimate reality, is the source and means of salvation.

Gnosticism is, in effect, a way of thinking that promises salvation to those who can accept it.

Salvation is through the awakening of true knowledge in the soul, mind, or spirit of the human receiver who comes to see, or know, that at her core, she is also spirit or mind and therefore is part or participant in the ultimate reality itself. Her lack of knowledge has led her into error, confusion, and imprisonment in less than divine realities, such as the lusts of the flesh and attachments to material and impermanent things.

The appeal of Gnosticism for early Christian thinkers was related to an increasing dissatisfaction with taking the biblical narrative at face value. The God of the Bible was portrayed in fairly straightforward terms as a singular personal agent, a being who created a material world in time and space and who acted within it. This was a divine being who in many ways shared a world with the human beings who inhabited it. But to many thinkers who had been imbued with the spirit of Platonism, this notion of a divine agent acting in history, time, and space began to seem too small, too anthropomorphic, and too limited to be taken as the supreme reality. Plato had bequeathed the notion of timelessness and immateriality as the characteristics of ultimacy. God had come to be affirmed as beyond time, space, and matter. Since the only thing humans had access to that was even close to being timeless, nonspatial, and immaterial were the ideas in the human mind, the access point to God became that of the mind. Mental objects (ideas) could not decay in time or degenerate through the corruptions of decaying matter. As forms of Platonism began to be accepted by early Christian thinkers (as a way of defending Christian belief in the face of rational attack by Greek philosophers), the notion of God as an agent was replaced by the notion of God as a reality far removed from the world of matter, space, and time. The human being was, by contrast, depicted as a lost, wandering soul, a spirit trapped in material conditions that threatened to cut the link between its true reality and the divine reality from which it ultimately had descended, or fallen. Gnostic thinking had developed a large number of stories or myths of symbolic allegories of how an immaterial Supreme Reality could have given rise to a material world. These stories had to be expressed in mythological or allegorical form because no human words or concepts could penetrate into and express the reality of God as God was in himself. Thus, different Gnostic thinkers had different mythological stories through which to portray the drama of the fall of humans into matter and redemption through saving knowledge.

Any religion that starts with the assumptions that God's ultimacy is beyond all human comprehension and finite limits and the fall of human beings into finitude and materiality, and the possibility of redemption or salvation from that fallen condition, will be attracted to some of the themes of Gnosticism. The question for the early Christians became one of the degree to which they could accept Gnostic themes without betraying the essential beliefs arising from the biblical picture of God's relationship to the world and its human inhabitants.

Gnosticism was not, strictly speaking, dualistic (as was the theology of Marcion, for example). Dualism postulated two equal and opposed divine forces, one purely spiritual and the other materialistic, or at least responsible for materiality. Gnosticism held to the view of one supreme God, out of whom or from whom the material world descended, usually through a series of intermediate steps caused by a struggle within the Godhead. The Gnostics tended to think of the original (and pure) form of the Godhead as one of a "fullness" (they used the word "pleroma") of beings, or Aeons, who comprised a kind of council surrounding, and worshiping by contemplation, the God at the center of the pleroma. This God was incomprehensible and could be known only partially by the various Aeons. But as the Christian bishop Valentinus wrote in his *Gospel of Truth*, one of the Aeons, Sophia, yearned to know more about the ultimate God (the Abyss or Forefather, who gave rise to the only begotten Father, the Beginning of all things) than she was permitted to. Only the Aeon known as the only begotten Mind was permitted to know the Father. When Sophia transgressed her appropriate limitations within the pleroma and discovered that this was impossible, her passion gave birth to a formless and shapeless thing, and she and it were expelled from the pleroma. The harmony of the pleroma was upset by Sophia's transgressions and passion, and a series of new Aeons emanated from within the pleroma in order to bring right knowledge of the pleroma and its relation to the Forefather to beings such as the expelled Sophia. This knowledge would allow them to return to the pleroma. Among these newly emanated Aeons are Christos and Jesus, whose job is to call to the spirits of the descendants of Sophia now trapped in matter and the world. Their spirits are to respond to the call of Jesus informed by Christos by becoming aware of their divine origin and rising above their material and earthly conditions.

The Gnostic assumption here is that there is a three-part division of humankind: the pneumatic or spiritual, the psychic or mental, and the hylic or material. Only the spiritual or pneumatic part of the human being will return to the pleroma in pure spiritual life characterized by contemplation of the oneness of all things.

Naturally, the early Christian motif of salvation from a world fallen into sin by a Savior, who was intimately linked to God and who brought the revelation of God's grace and mercy to that world, was seen by many as having some relationship with modes of Gnostic thought. If God were thought of as extremely far away from human reality, some kind of intermediary or go-between would be necessary if humans were ever to "return" to the source from which they came. The 40 days Jesus spent with disciples after his resurrection are when most Gnostics think he revealed esoteric teachings about how human beings were to be saved.

In these Gnostic conceptions, Jesus was seen primarily as a teacher, an imparter of wisdom, rather than as someone who redeemed humankind by dying on a cross as punishment for human sin.

With Christians struggling to define who Jesus was in relation to themselves and to God, Gnostic leanings were almost inevitable. Christians of all stripes saw Jesus as in some sense an intermediary, a mediator, between God and human beings. The struggle at Nicaea, of course, was over how to define or articulate the kind of mediator Jesus was, and Gnosticism was at least an influence on some bishops at the council.

But there were going to be supreme obstacles to Christians accepting the full panoply of Gnostic teachings. Chief among these was the biblical belief that God (the true and ultimate God) had created the world directly. And that world was decidedly material, spatial, and temporal, and at its creation God called it "good." Some believed that the instrument God used in creation was wisdom or Spirit, but it was still a creation for which God was ultimately responsible.

Another obstacle in Gnostic thinking that the early Christians had to confront was the tendency among Gnostics to think that the material body of Jesus was at best a disguise or cloak that concealed his real, and spiritual, being. This put the Gnostics fairly close to the Docetists, who also rejected the notion of God in human form. Many Christians thought God had to be in human form (incarnate, meaning "in flesh") in order for Jesus's sacrifice to atone for sin.

A third obstacle for Christians in accepting Gnosticism was the latter's insistence that the problem of suffering in the world was caused by a lack of saving knowledge. Many Christians would insist that suffering resulted from the sinful and erring will of the human being. It was not lack of knowledge but lack of right intention that put people at odds with God. Gnosticism had a tendency to exempt persons from personal sin since they were not responsible for their plight: it was the fault of the wayward Aeons, who had disturbed the pleroma and fallen into materiality and the world. Nevertheless, most Gnostics insisted on a highly ascetic form of life simply because detachment from worldly things prepared the spirit to receive the *gnosis* from God through the intermediation of Jesus Christ. Ironically, many Gnostics were indifferent to the physical bodies of their fellow believers since bodies and genders were irrelevant to the spirit. As a result, they had little problem with women being equal participants or even leaders (bishops) in their communities, a position at odds with the majority of bishops, who insisted that bishops be men since Jesus was a man. Gnostics also were not interested in remembering Jesus's death (since the "true" Jesus never died, never having had a body essential to his identity in the first place). Much of the opposition to Gnosticism had to do with the failure of Gnostics to accept the full authority of the bishops of the Church, many of whom they rejected because they were too focused on "earthly" things rather than the things of the spirit.

Nevertheless, despite these obstacles, Gnostic forms of thinking did attract Christian thinkers, and it is believed that there are echoes (or perhaps even a foreshadowing) of Gnostic thinking in the Gospel of John and in the writings of the apostle Paul. (See 1 Corinthians 1:24, where Paul speaks of Christ, the power of God, and the wisdom of God.) In the Gospel of John, the Son of Man is referred to both as the Logos, or Word of God, and as the Glory of God, a phrase that some have taken as reminiscent of Gnostic ideas. Neither the apostle Paul nor the apostle John were in fact Gnostics, but there is enough in some of the phrasing used by them and other early Christian writers to suggest some similarities with Gnostic thinking.

At the Council of Nicaea, there were some bishops who were inclined toward Gnosticism and were trying to find a way to incorporate their Gnostic leanings into the language of the creed.

The chief opponent of the Gnostics was Irenaeus, bishop of Lyons, who wrote a text called *Adversus Haereses*, or *Against Heresies*, at the end of the second century, which attacked Gnosticism as a heresy.

But even Irenaeus had a hierarchy of Gods from the ultimate God to the lower manifestation of God (the Word or Son) and the Spirit (who works in the world). His world was less populated with Aeons than were those of Valentinus and the Gnostics, but it assumed what they did: that God himself was incomprehensible and required the mediation of multiple divine beings to reveal himself.

Certainly, the bishops at Nicaea knew Irenaeus's work and were going to be careful to steer clear of outright endorsement of Gnostic beliefs even though some of the bishops were clearly sympathetic to them.

SOURCES

Brakke, David. *The Gnostics*. Cambridge, MA: Harvard University Press, 2010.

Eliade, Mircea, ed. "Gnosticism," in *Encyclopedia of Religion*. New York: Macmillan, 1987.

Filoramo, Giovanni. *A History of Gnosticism*. Oxford: Blackwell, 1992.

Jonas, Hans. *The Gnostic Religion*. Boston: Beacon, 1968.

Appendix 2. Calendars and the Date to Celebrate the Resurrection

The Roman Empire used the Julian calendar developed by Julius Caesar in 44 B.C.E., which was modified in 8 B.C.E. by Augustus to give his month, August, as many days as July, named for Julius.[1] This was a vast improvement over the previous calendar, which was constantly being adjusted to try to keep it synchronized with the seasons and was subject to malicious manipulation by the officials whose job it was to define each year. The Julian calendar had 365¼ days, as does our modern calendar, and was accurate enough that it produced an error of only 1 day every 128 years. It persisted until the sixteenth century, when it was adjusted by Pope Gregory to correct 1600 years of these accumulated errors.

The Julian calendar used six months of 31 days: January, March, May, July, September, and November. The other months had 30 days, except February, which normally had 29 days. Augustus took one more day away from February and added it to August, giving it 31 days as well.

The Julian calendar was sufficiently accurate that the positions of the equinoxes in the spring and fall were stable. However, astronomical measurements were poor enough that there was a discrepancy in various parts of the empire as to which day in March marked the spring equinox, the twenty-first or the twenty-third.

Each month was divided into sections. The first day of the month was designated the Kalends and was the day when debts were due. The infamous Ides was the thirteenth day of the month, except in March, May, July, and October, when it was the fifteenth. The Nones occurred eight days before the Ides, so it was either the fifth or the seventh day of the month. The days between these fixed days were counted as the number of days until the next named day.

Using the Julian calendar, the spring equinox would have occurred on XI Kalends April (eleven days before the first of April, or March 21). Saturnalia began on XVI Kalends January (December 17) and often extended for seven days, until IX Kalends January (December 23).

The idea of a seven-day week has its roots in ancient Babylon and was used by the Jews throughout their history. Genesis has God working for six days of creation and resting on the seventh. Christians followed the same schedule. The Roman week was not based on the seven days until 321 C.E., when Constantine decreed it would be used throughout the empire.

THE JEWISH CALENDAR

The Jewish calendar is more sophisticated and complex than the Roman calendar in that it uses all of the motions of the earth, sun, and moon.[2] Although both calendars use the word "month," which derives from the motion of the moon, the Roman calendar abandoned any attempt to use the lunar rotation as part of its system. Since the moon orbits around the earth on average every 29.4 days, a single year may contain either 12 or 13 new moons and thus either 12 or 13 months. Thus, two different kinds of years must be defined to account for this.

Hillel II (c.320–365 C.E.) is thought to have fixed the Jewish calendar so that religious leaders did not need to determine the corrections and leap years and months. His calendar is based on a 19-year cycle. In seven of these years, an extra month of Adar is added to make a 13-month year. The months, which always begin with the new moon, have either 29 or 30 days. Six months—Nissan, Sivan, Av, Tishri, Shevat, and Adar I—always have 30 days. Five months—Iyar, Tammuz, Elul, Tevet, and Adar II (Adar II in leap years)—always have 29 days. The other months, Cheshvan and Kislev, which occur in the fall, have either 29 or 30 days. The actual determination of whether these months have 29 or 30 days is based on observations of the time when the new moon occurs. Students interested in the full mathematical details of the calendar are referred to the reference in note 2 of this appendix.

It should be noted that the new moon used for the start of the month is not the astronomical new moon but a calculated new moon. Hillel did this to synchronize the month so that it would always match the average lunar month.

The Jewish New Year occurs in the month of Tishri in the fall. Tishri is the most critical month in terms of establishing the overall calendar. The length of the leap months depends on the time of day at which the full moon occurs in the month of Tishri in the coming year and the day of the week on which 1 Tishri would occur in the following year. Therefore, one must look forward a year to determine the calendar for the current year. Because the two months after Tishri can vary in length and there is the possible addition of the extra month of Adar, determining when Passover occurs is complex.

Because Jesus was crucified during Passover, early Christians celebrated the Resurrection on the third day after the start of Passover. This meant the Resurrection feast was not always on Sunday. Later, most Christians moved the celebration to the Sunday after the start of Passover so that the Resurrection celebration would always occur on Sunday. Figuring out when to celebrate the Resurrection is not trivial.

The proper date to celebrate the Resurrection was a significant issue for the Council of Nicaea and is the source of ongoing confusion for Christians today, as Easter moves through March and April. The council will almost certainly maintain the tradition that Resurrection day occurs on Sunday. Setting the date to be synchronized with Passover will require that bishops become experts on the Hillel calendar. Alternatively, they may devise another system based on the lunar cycle, possibly taking into account the spring equinox to make things simpler. The simplest option would be to use a fixed date.

The Jewish calendar was considerably more accurate than the Julian calendar. The Julian calendar required an additional day of correction every 128 years. The Jewish calendar requires a correction of one day about every 300 years. You are all quite capable of working your way to the day of the week of your birthday 20 years from now, but none of us could casually determine the date to celebrate the Resurrection of Jesus two years from now.

The council will probably be split on this issue. Constantine would like to have a fixed date for the convenience of the people, and he would like it to be close to the equinox since this is already a holiday in the empire and will make it easy for people to adjust to being Christians. The more anti-Jewish bishops will probably support this as a way to reduce connections to Judaism in the Church. But another major group will argue that the theology of Christ as the Paschal lamb of God and the connection this makes with Passover requires that the observance of Pascha remain linked to the lunar calendar even if it is a modified version that is simpler than the true Jewish calendar.

Appendix 3. The Doctrine of the Trinity

The development of the doctrines about the nature of Jesus cannot be separated from the development of what the Christians came to call the doctrine of the Trinity. This is surely one of the doctrines or articles of faith that are the most complex and difficult to comprehend in all of Christian theology.

At its core are two fundamental convictions that are not easily harmonized with each other. First is the conviction, drawn from the Hebraic scriptures and the experience of the Jewish people, that God is a personal agent who has acted in a multitude of ways in the temporal, spatial, and material world, and more specifically in the lives of the Jewish people themselves over the course of human history. This conviction was reflected in the daily prayers, worship, and liturgical life of the various communities of Christians in the years after the death of Jesus. It is what we might call an "experiential conviction." The other conviction, drawn primarily from Greek or Hellenistic philosophy and understood as the "metaphysical conviction," is that God is absolutely transcendent of time, space, and matter and cannot, by virtue of his own divine nature, have any contact with the empirical world.

The doctrine of the Trinity was developed over time out of various attempts to put these two convictions into a coherent relationship with each other. It is important to note that just as the ideas about Jesus that were debated at Nicaea were not articulated precisely in scripture (and for this reason gave rise to contrasting points of view, all of which could claim authority from scripture), so the convictions that would eventually coalesce into the doctrine of the Trinity are not precisely and clearly explicated in scripture. Those who eventually adopted and embraced the doctrine of the Trinity would naturally claim that the doctrine was always implicit and presupposed in scripture.

At the heart of the doctrine of the Trinity is the place of Jesus, and somewhat secondarily the role of the Holy Spirit. Not only was it important to state *for* human beings who Jesus was but also to state what *his* relation to God was. The doctrine of the Trinity emerges, in part, from the *experience* of the early Christians that Jesus was related to God in some way that went beyond or was qualitatively different from the way God was related to other human beings or to the world in general. In or through Jesus (especially his death and resurrection from the dead), the Christians felt that they had been redeemed from their sinfulness, saved from eternal damnation, and reconciled with God. Jesus was clearly instrumental, in their experience, in that redemption, reconciliation, and salvation. Early Christians, even without a fully developed theology, had called Jesus "Lord," an appellation that they would give to no ordinary human being but only to God himself. Something in their experience of Jesus marked him as different from other human beings (though he was clearly human) and at the same time as having a special kind of relationship with God. There was no language available in the third century to put this experience into words. In fact, the doctrine of the Trinity is best seen as a series of attempts over time to take a primordial experience by Christians of a relationship with Jesus and to put it into language that both reflected that experience faithfully and made sense intellectually.

The primordial experience for the Christians was one of experiencing God as being over them, with them, and in them. And, following the Jewish model, there was one and only one God who could relate to them in all these ways. Three deities (tritheism) was never a theological option for the Christians, as it clearly could not have been for Jews. One way that the early Christians tried to express the oneness of God and the multiplicity of human experiences of God was through what has been called the "economy" (*oikonomia*) of redemption. This refers to the different modes of expression or activity of God. God creates, God redeems or saves, and God inspires (literally, "in-spirits"). As Father, God is creator of all things other than himself; as Jesus, God redeems and saves humankind; and as Holy Spirit, God inspires, comforts, or dwells in each person. These distinct activities suggested that in God there were at least some distinctions that could be identified because they had been *experienced* as distinct. The creation of the world was an act distinct from the redemption of humankind, which in turn was an act distinct from the way in which God dwells in each human being to inspire and to comfort. They were *experiential* distinctions for Christians, though in God they were one because God was one. But these economical distinctions did not imply an ontological (or reality-based) distinction, hence a distinction of functions with no distinction in the nature of the reality that was experienced as functionally distinct.

The debate at Nicaea was centered on the question of whether a human being (perhaps *similar* in nature to God) could affect redemption or whether this was such a radically powerful act that it required God's own activity to accomplish. Before the fourth century, almost all Christians assumed that Jesus was in some sense subordinate to God even though he was the vehicle or means through which God accomplished the salvation of persons. It was Arius who pushed the issue of whether Jesus's nature, as a human being, necessarily had to be different in some way from the nature of God the Father. As long as Jesus was understood to be begotten or derived from God the Father, he was not therefore automatically assumed to be of exactly the same nature as God. But the conviction of the Christians was that Jesus, to accomplish the work of salvation, had to be of the same nature as God since only God (not one of his created agents) has the power to save. What needed saving was human nature, and therefore no mere

human being, no matter how perfect, could save the very nature of which he himself was made.

The problem was how to define or describe the relations *within* God between the economic manifestations *of* God. God was clearly uncreated, unoriginated, and unbegotten. However, Jesus in some sense had been begotten of the Father from all eternity (not created in time) and thus was in some sense distinct from the Father while at the same time being of the same nature as the Father so as to be the Father's power, or Word, of redemption.

One of the more difficult issues the doctrine of the Trinity had to address was whether, in his economic activity as Son, God suffered as Jesus suffered on the cross. This was the problem known as "patripassionism": the passion or suffering of the Father. Greek or Hellenistic philosophy (into which Christian theology was attempting to fit its ideas) had no place for a notion of God suffering. God's very nature (related to the second conviction on which the doctrine of the Trinity was built) was believed to be beyond time, space, and matter: it was impassive and immutable (that is, incapable of changing in any respect). This meant that when Christians talked about God appearing in the form of a human being (Jesus), such talk must necessarily be paradoxical or literally illogical. The formal doctrine of the Trinity was an attempt to move beyond paradox into a language about God that, although mysterious, made sense in theological terms.

The place of the Holy Spirit in the Trinity clearly came after the relation between Jesus and the Father had generally been worked out. Christians were already baptizing in the name of the Spirit, but its fuller meaning emerged with the work of Irenaeus (c.200 C.E.), who talked about the Spirit primarily as the wisdom of God by which God created. It is only through the wisdom implanted in us that we are able to understand the work of God in and through Jesus. The Spirit provided the plan of creation, and the Word carried the plan for the Father into its execution in the world. The Spirit was also called the Paraclete, the one who comforts the faithful, intercedes for them, teaches, helps, and advocates before the Father for those who are faithful.

One faction of early Christians (loosely grouped in what is called Gnosticism) developed this notion of God's radical difference from human beings to the point of rejecting human nature. They pushed the second conviction to its logical conclusion: if God is immutable, impassible, and nonmaterial, then God can have no contact with or involvement in the temporal, spatial, and material world. Therefore, any God who created matter would have to be contaminated by it. The Gnostics (the word comes from "knowledge" or secret teaching) believed that the true and essential nature of human beings was nonmaterial spirit. They repudiated any notion of an Incarnation, in which God takes on human form. Jesus, for them, was a divine spirit who only seemed to be human, wearing a human disguise (his body), which he shed at the moment of the crucifixion. His purpose, before his death, was to provide knowledge to the spirits of those other persons (also trapped within material bodies) of the destiny of all spirits, a destiny in a nonmaterial, purely spiritual realm. God did not become less than fully spirit and did not suffer, so the Gnostics avoided the problem of patripassionism. They were suspicious of any attempt to think about Jesus as having an essential human nature, especially a bodily nature.

Gnosticism was a larger phenomenon in this period, going beyond Christian communities. The dualism between God and the material world and between good and evil was common. Some Gnostic communities devised elaborate mythologies. Whether Christian Gnostics accepted all of them is not clear, but Gnosticism was a live option for many early Christians during the years before a Christian creed had been developed. The Gnostics themselves did not constitute a single organized group and were not, at the outset, outside the mainstream of Christian theology. They only became so as the result of various councils and creeds of the Church in the fourth century and later. What the orthodox position ultimately could not accept were the Gnostic claims that the true God did not create the world directly but used a lesser being to do so (the God of the Old Testament), did not have direct involvement in it, was not incarnated in Jesus, did not die on the cross, and was not resurrected bodily from the dead.

Notes

1. INTRODUCTION

1. Both Nicaea and Nicea are used as spellings for this council. The former produces richer search results in most search engines and is used here.

2. HISTORICAL BACKGROUND

1. Tabor, *Jesus Dynasty*, 65.

2. Full text available at http://www.newadvent .org/fathers/0311.htm, accessed January 7, 2015.

3. Tertullian, *Prescription against Heretics*, chapter 16, http://www.newadvent.org/fathers/0311 .htm, accessed January 7, 2015.

4. Derived from J. T. Lienhard, *The Arian Controversy: Some Categories Reconsidered*, and from Everett Ferguson, ed., *The Doctrines of God and Christ in the Early Church*, p. 415.

5. The term "incarnation," or God incarnate, derives from the Latin and means literally "in meat."

6. Ferguson, *The Doctrines of God and Christ*, p. 426.

7. The King James Version was first published in 1611 and is based on Greek and Hebrew texts available at the time.

8. The Revised Standard Version (RSV) is a translation of the Bible that employed nineteenth- and twentieth-century biblical scholarship in an effort to reconstruct the early text of the New Testament. Thus, it differs from the King James Version from the seventeenth century.

9. The history is based on Kousoulas (1997), Rubenstein (1999), and other sources.

10. See http://www.fourthcentury.com/index .php/urkunde-18 for a detailed account of this council.

3. THE GAME

1. The term "Easter" developed long after the Council of Nicaea. It comes from the Old English word "Ēastre" or "Ēostre," originally referring to the name of the Anglo-Saxon goddess "Ēostre" (see Barnhart 1995).

2. Eusebius, *Life of Constantine*, quoted from http://www.newadvent.org/fathers/25023.htm, accessed April 3, 2015.

APPENDIX 2

1. Information found at http://www.geocities .com/calendopaedia/julian.htm, accessed July 22, 2006 C.E.

2. See http://www.jewfaq.org/calendr2.htm, accessed July 22, 2006 C.E. [26 Tammuz 5766].

References Cited

Barnhart, Robert K. *The Barnhart Concise Dictionary of Etymology*. New York: HarperCollins, 1995.

Brown, Dan. *The DaVinci Code*. New York: Doubleday, 2003.

Chadwick, Henry. *The Role of the Christian Bishop in Ancient Society*, ed. Edward C. Hobbs and Wilhelm Wuellner, The Center for Hermeneutical Studies in Hellenistic and Modern Culture. Berkeley: The Graduate Theological Union and the University of California, 1979.

Crossan, John D., and Jonathan L. Reed. *In Search of Paul*. San Francisco: HarperCollins, 2004.

Ehrman, Bart. *Jesus—Apocalyptic Prophet of the New Millennium*. New York: Oxford University Press, 1999.

———. *Lost Christianities*. New York: Oxford University Press, 2003.

———. *Misquoting Jesus*. San Francisco: Harper, 2005.

Eusebius [of Caesarea]. *The History of the Church*. http://www.ccel.org/ccel/schaff/npnf201, accessed November 10, 2013.

———. *Life of Constantine*. http://www.fordham.edu/halsall/basis/vita-constantine.asp, accessed May 12, 2016.

Ferguson, Everett, ed. *The Doctrines of God and Christ in the Early Church*. London: Taylor and Francis, 1951.

Freke, Timothy, and Peter Gandy. *The Jesus Mysteries: Was the "Original Jesus" a Pagan God?* New York: Three Rivers, 1999.

Gonzalez, J. L. *Story of Christianity*, vol. 1. San Francisco: Harper and Row, 1984.

Hippolytus of Rome. *The Apostolic Tradition*, trans. Kevin P. Edgecomb. http://www.bombaxo.com/hippolytus.html, accessed November 10, 2013.

Jones, A. H. M. *The Later Roman Empire*. New York: Oxford University Press, 1964.

Josephus. *Antiquities of the Jews*. http://sacred-texts.com/jud/josephus/ant-pref.htm, accessed February 20, 2014.

Klostermaier, Klaus. *A Survey of Hinduism*, Second Edition. Albany: SUNY Albany Press, 1994.

Kousoulas, D. G. *The Life and Times of Constantine the Great*. Danbury, CT: Rutledge, 1997.

Latin Vulgate Bible with Translation. "The First Epistle of St. John the Apostle," chapter 5. http://www.latinvulgate.com/lv/verse.aspx?t=1&b=23&c=5, accessed November 4, 2013.

Lienhard, Joseph T., S.J. "The Arian Controversy: Some Categories Reconsidered," in *Studies in Early Christianity*, vol. 9: *Doctrines of God and Christ in the Early Church*, ed. Everett Ferguson, pp. 87–109. New York: Garland, 1993.

MacCulloch, Diarmaid. *Christianity—The First Three Thousand Years*. New York: Viking, 2010.

Metzger, Bruce M. "Explicit References in the Works of Origen to Variant Readings in New Testament Manuscripts," in *Historical and Literary Studies: Pagan, Jewish, and Christian*. Grand Rapids, MI: Eerdmans, 1968.

Pagels, Elaine. *Beyond Belief: The Secret Gospel of Thomas*. New York: Random House, 2003.

———. *The Gnostic Gospels*. New York: Vintage, 1989.

———. *The Gnostic Paul*. Peabody, MA: Trinity Press International, 1975.

Qur'an. Sahai Translation. http://quran.com/4, accessed November 3, 2013.

Rubinstein, R. E. *When Jesus Became God*. Orlando, FL: Harcourt, 1999.

Sanders, E. P. *Judaism Practice and Belief, 63 BCE—66 CE*. Peabody, MA: Trinity Press International, 1992.

Stephenson, Paul. *Constantine—Roman Emperor, Christian Victor*. New York: Overlook, 2010.

Tabor, James. *The Jesus Dynasty*. New York: Simon and Schuster, 2006.

Tertullian. *The Prescription against Heretics*, in *Early Christian Writings*, trans. Rev. Peter Holmes, ed. Peter Kirby. http://www.earlychristianwritings.com/text/tertullian11.html, accessed March 31, 2016.

Wilson, Barrie. *How Jesus Became Christian*. New York: St. Martin's, 2008.

9 781469 631417